Writing for the Stage
THE PLAYWRIGHT'S HANDBOOK

Writing for the Stage
THE PLAYWRIGHT'S HANDBOOK

Anthony Clark

THE CROWOOD PRESS

First published in 2021 by
The Crowood Press Ltd
Ramsbury, Marlborough
Wiltshire SN8 2HR

enquiries@crowood.com

www.crowood.com

British Library Cataloguing-in-Publication Data
A catalogue record for this book is available from the British Library.

ISBN 978 1 78500 902 0

Frontispiece: Nick Sidi in *Taking Care of Baby* (2007) by Dennis Kelly. Premiered at The Door,
Birminham Rep. Photograph: Robert Day

Disclaimer
Every reasonable effort has been made to trace and credit illustration copyright holders.
If you own the copyright to an image appearing in this book and have not been credited,
please contact the publisher, who will be pleased to add a credit in any future edition.

Typeset by Simon and Sons

Cover design by Maggie Mellett

Printed and bound in India by Replika Press Pvt Ltd

CONTENTS

DEDICATION

This book is dedicated to all the playwrights I have worked with and students I have taught who have convinced me of the important role theatre can play in shaping the life of the individual and, therefore, the evolution of society.

ACKNOWLEDGEMENTS

I would like to thank the following for their help in preparing this book: Delia Goddard for patiently putting up with me talking through the contents of each chapter; designer Jessica Curtis for letting me include her design drawings, and Nicola Clark, Ruari Murchison, Ian Tilton, Robert Day and Tristram Kenton for their generous help with the photographs.

ILLUSTRATION CREDITS

Robert Day: pages 8, 24, 61 (bottom left), 63 (top), 75, 82 and 124
Tristram Kenton: pages 12, 28, 32, 38, 59, 61 (top left), 63 (bottom), 66, 78 (both), 85, 106, 131 and 136
Delia Goddard: page 15
Kevin Ung: pages 22 and 120

ABOUT THE AUTHOR

Anthony Clark read Drama at Manchester University, following a BA Hons degree with a Post-Graduate Diploma in Playwriting. He is currently working as freelance director and playwright, as well as course leader for MA Directing, and MA Dramatic Writing at Drama Centre at Central Saint Martins. He also has his own company, Theatre Accord. Previous posts include: artistic director of Hampstead Theatre (2003–10), associate artistic director, Birmingham Rep (1997–2002), associate director, Birmingham Rep (1990–97), artistic director, Contact Theatre (1984–90) and assistant director, Orange Tree Theatre (1981–83). He has freelanced extensively, working with companies that include The National, RSC, Young Vic, Bristol Old Vic, Leicester Haymarket, Nottingham Playhouse and Tara Arts.

His recent plays include: *Paradise of the Assassins* (Theatre Accord National Tour, 2016), *Our Brother David* (Watford Palace, 2012), *Naked Not Nude* (Linbury Studio LAMDA [London Academy of Music and Dramatic Arts], 2014 and Platform Theatre, Central Saint Martins, 2018), *The Eighth Continent* (Tristan Bates, 2013). Earlier plays include: *The Power of Darkness* trans. Tolstoy (The Orange Tree, 1983), *Wake* (The Orange Tree, 1983), *Tide Mark* (RSC Pit, Thought Crimes Festival, 1984), *Green* (Contact Theatre, 1985), *Matter of Life and Death* (50th Anniversary Lorca, Lyttleton Theatre, NT, 1986). And several adaptations for children, including: *The Little Prince* (Contact Theatre, 1986), the award-winning *Red Balloon* (Contact, 1990; Bristol Old Vic, 1991; Olivier Theatre, NT, 1996), *The Pied Piper* (1993), *Pinocchio* (1996), *Winnie The Witch* (Birmingham Rep., 2001), *Little Wolf's Book of Badness* (Hampstead Theatre, 2007). Several of his plays have been published and produced throughout Britain and internationally. *The Red Balloon* was produced as a Boxing Day Special on Radio 4.

INTRODUCTION

The theatre is an essential art form that is forever evolving. My observations about playwriting are based on my work as a professional director and playwright, and as an artistic director of three theatres in the UK over the past forty years. I have always had a particular interest in giving opportunities to emerging playwrights, as well as producing new plays by more established writers. In recent years I have enjoyed leading an MA course on playwriting for Central Saint Martins, the University of the Arts, London. I have also written, had produced and published a number of original plays and adaptations for a range of different audiences. I like to think I know something of the tremendous effort that goes into writing for the stage, and the challenges the playwright faces in trying to get their work produced.

This book is not a history book about the evolution of playwriting. It will be an introduction to emerging playwrights and a reminder to others of some of the skills needed to write a play. It is not a definitive manual, because stage conventions go in and out of fashion, as the content and context in which plays are produced changes. It is not a book of rules. There will always be successful plays that emerge that don't adhere to any of the rules that practitioners and academics identify as essential to playwriting. No teacher is infallible. My aim is to help you to understand something of the art and craft of writing for the stage and to avoid some of the pitfalls. It is to encourage you to make the most of the medium,

and to enjoy writing stories in dialogue that speak directly to the times in which you are writing. Different theatre companies' commissioning and programming imperatives change constantly in response to public taste and funding priorities. It is important to keep up to speed with what is happening by going to the theatre regularly, reading as many plays as you can and trawling the industry websites.

Given my experience of programming, producing and directing, I will also look at the role of the playwright in the production process.

It is not within the scope of this book to explore in any depth the work of playwrights not writing in the English language. I would urge you, however, if you are serious about developing your craft as a writer, to look at what has been, and is being, achieved by playwrights and theatre-makers in other parts of the world. Keep up with any visiting international touring programmes, and the work presented at prestigious international theatre festivals. Details of which are all available online.

Throughout the book, the 'you' I refer to will be 'you' the playwright.

I started writing plays whilst at Manchester University doing a BA in Drama because I was enthused by the way my teachers taught the subject, the energy and talents of my peers, and I felt passionately about what was going on in the world at the time. It was the late 1970s, a time of punk, the east and the west were still building their nuclear arsenals, racism was rife in all walks of life, and second-wave feminism was making me think about the cultural and political inequalities women faced. I felt I had political things to say and I wanted to see certain things happen on stage that I believed had never been done

OPPOSITE: Gregor Henderson-Begg and Alan Rothwell in the premiere of Philip Ridley's *Krindlekrax* (2002) at the Nottingham Playhouse.

before. I wanted to create the story and to control the story. Looking back, I have to admit that my knowledge of what had been done, and what was being done, on stage at the time was negligible. All fired up, I wrote and directed my first play at nineteen, a domestic tragicomedy called *The Wall*. It was set somewhere non-specific, involving a series of arguments that divided a family of four in two. I can't remember what their initial falling out was all about, but maybe that was the point. In the course of the play, the characters dismantled the back wall of their kitchen, which was made up of roughly painted cardboard boxes, and rebuilt it across the room… as a crude metaphorical representation of what was literally happening to them. They built it over the kitchen table, so that the two sides couldn't contact each other. It was a naive allegory, perhaps, for The Berlin Wall, which separated East and West Germany at the time. I remember very little about it other than that one side of the family eventually found a way to communicate with the other by talking under the table.

I'm sure the play was not a good read, but it played well according to the reviews. The success of a play is not measured on how well it reads, but on how well it comes across in performance. The playwright is dependent on a range of collaborators for this.

As well as exploring some of the mechanics of playwriting in this book, I have identified who these collaborators might be, and the playwright's relationship to them. The alchemy that occurs when a group of theatre artists and practitioners focus intensely on a particular production is amazing. The opportunity to put the results in front of an audience can be truly exhilarating.

Plays like poems concentrate experience.

At the same time as globalization is leading playwrights, amongst others, to explore how far experience can be said to be universal, the obligation in the UK to diversify audiences through the promotion of culturally specific, authentic work that celebrates 'difference', is growing. So that these two imperatives don't work in opposition to each other, playwrights might do well to take their cue from visual artists and musicians, who have for years thrived on synthesizing cultural influences in their practice. In the theatre, however, audiences and critics are quick to accuse playwrights and practitioners who do this of cultural appropriation, of not fully understanding the context and significance of the material they are using. I, personally, am excited by an eclectic approach to production and new forms of theatre emerging through cultural synthesis. That said, I believe playwrights should use whatever means they think appropriate to speak to their target audience.

Whilst I have been writing this book the whole world has been in the grip of a global pandemic and has had to do what it can to slow down the spread of Covid-19. Theatres in the UK have been closed for the past six months, and although some outdoor theatres and a few indoor venues, where it is financially viable to perform with safe distancing, have managed to reopen, the industry shows no sign of returning to 'business as usual' for the foreseeable future. Covid-19 has been devastating for theatre artists, with many losing regular employment and a vast number of freelancers losing opportunities to work. My own new play *She*, which was due to do a national tour this autumn (2020), has had to be postponed for a year. In response to the crisis, many theatre companies have broadcast old productions online, and many individual artists have entered the digital realm to participate in the creation of stories that reflect the human condition back to humanity. People around the world have turned to the creative sector for entertainment and guidance. The online initiatives, however ingenious and good, are no substitute for live performance. Those of us involved in the creation of theatre, and those who hanker to see it, are missing the human scale, the thrill, the joy and reassurance, of the collective live event – entering the space as an individual and becoming part of an audience.

Theatre is about the great art of living together, and post-Covid-19, I hope people of differing ages and backgrounds will once again come together at the same time, in the same space, to experience the same sequence of events and arguments, and to walk away entertained and enlightened.

Anthony Clark
September 2020

1
WHAT IS A PLAY?

I regard the theatre as the greatest of all art forms, the most immediate way in which a human being can share with another the sense of what it is to be a human being.

Oscar Wilde (1854–1900)

Ever since humankind evolved to communicate, we have been using storytelling to pass on knowledge, and rituals to connect with others and help us come to terms with, and control, the unknown. Plays happened, when storytelling combined with ritual.

It is impossible to be definitive about what a play is. Suffice to say that at an impressive performance of a play, the participants, both the actors and the audience, will experience consciously and subconsciously, the purpose and power of art.

The purpose of art being to confirm or better our understanding of the world. The power of art being to ravish our senses and stimulate our intellect.

A play is a distillation of actions, thoughts and feelings derived from real life, expressed in dialogue and stage directions, by a playwright or group of theatre-makers, for the entertainment of an audience or readers. A play can make us laugh or cry or both. It can confirm what we already know or it can introduce us to new worlds. It can relax us or incite us to action. It can, of course, do a combination of all or any of these at the same time.

The form and content of a play is determined by its historical context. A theatre-maker's initial response to the world may be an emotional one. Then, with a learnt or instinctive curiosity, some

will want to investigate why they feel the way they do and share their discoveries with an audience, whilst others will be more concerned to find a way to generate a comparable emotional response in the audience and leave them to derive meaning from it. If they are interested in cause and effect drama, then the chances are that the playwright will construct a linear narrative. If not, they may choose a more expressionistic, non-linear form. Both approaches invite the audience or reader to reflect on their own experience.

More often than not, a play, like any work of fiction, is an inventive construction of an imaginary world inspired by the real world. It needs to be sufficiently informed by your own experience for us to empathize with the plight of the characters, to follow the narrative and be challenged or reassured by the ideas contained therein. At some level, the audience will always need to recognize something of the world of the play to make sense of it.

For centuries people talked about 'hearing' plays and then they talked about 'seeing' them, as the theatre strove, using whatever means it could, to make the action more visible and the spectacle more impressive. The descriptive panorama of Elizabethan action, conjured in the imagination through language, gradually gave way to representation of reality that would fit the 'picture-frame stage'. As an aesthetic, realism still dominates theatrical presentation, because it is the easiest to relate to. In the first half of the twenty-first

OPPOSITE: Caroline Faber and David Kennedy in Abi Morgan's *Tender*.

Tripti Tripuraneni, Rani Fantania, Asif Khan and Skye Hallam in rehearsal for *Paradise of the Assassins* (2016) by Anthony Clark based on the book by Abdul Halim Sharar.

century, with the popularity of 'site-specific' and 'immersive' theatre, and the blurring of the lines between 'drama' and 'performance art', people have started to talk about going to 'experience' a play. Plays are often performed in non-traditional, flexible venues. There is even a theatre for the 'connected generation' in virtual space, which incorporates various social networks into the production and presentation of shows.

For many years, plays in UK theatres have been patronized by the people who have the time and the money to spend on them. As a result, the stories presented have tended to reflect the concerns of a particular demographic – the prosperous middle-class. There are theatre companies, however, led by artists who are not driven by the commercial imperative to make a profit but by a strong belief that theatre can play a vital role in the

integration of society and contribute to the well-being of the individual, who have striven for years, and are still striving, for a more inclusive theatre. By choosing a wider range of stories and presenting them in less familiar forms at affordable prices, these companies do what they can to ensure access to under-privileged, minority groups of artists and audiences. Supported by public funding, a number of trusts and foundations, and contributions from philanthropic donors, they are targeting new audiences and extending the boundaries of the art form.

As our understanding and appreciation of global diversity increases, so does recognition of our common concerns; for example, the effects of climate change, the inequities of capitalism, religious fundamentalism, racism, identity, gender, the role of the individual in society and so on. Our plays need to address these concerns across constituencies within our communities, and globally. Our future and the future of the planet will be determined by what unites us, not what divides us. This approach over time will inform what is popular and commercial.

WHY ARE PLAYS CALLED PLAYS?

It is no accident that plays are called plays. To be able to play is essential to our development from childhood to adulthood and to our evolution as a species. To play is instinctive. It is the means whereby we reflect on our own experience to make sense of it, and on the experiences of others. It is also how we experiment with what 'might be'.

Our individual survival is dependent on our ability to integrate with others, and our route to integration is to acknowledge what we do and don't share with them. Witnessing a play can offer us the opportunity to explore known and imagined circumstances. It allows us to rehearse life experience in a safe place – a place where we can test, objectively, certain truths; a place where different constituencies within the community can explore their differences, or have their identities reaffirmed. We are a species that needs to understand each other and who we are.

WRITING FOR LIVE PERFORMANCE

There are many similarities between writing a play for live performance and other media, but there are

Poster for *Playing by the Rules* (1994) by Rod Dungate, a first play commissioned and produced in the Door at Birmingham Rep.

also some significant differences. Across all media, if you are interested in narrative, you have to have a story that is plotted to reveal your themes. Interest in your story will be maintained, primarily, through your ability to generate tension. Tension is generated by you charting carefully when to reveal what happens to your characters and why it happens.

Characters reveal themselves through their ability to initiate and respond to what is going on. What is going on, where and when, establishes a play's atmosphere. Tension is maintained by a play's atmosphere.

It is assumed that characters on screen can be presented more subtly than those on stage and, therefore, if you want to write 'big', 'loud', 'demonstrative' characters, then write for the stage. It is also assumed that if your story requires many different locations, this could present an insurmountable challenge to a theatre production team. Again, not necessarily the case.

In film, you tell your story primarily through action and visuals.

In TV, like writing for the stage, your story and themes unravel primarily through dialogue, although action and visuals are, of course, important.

For audio, radio and podcasts, your story is told entirely through sounds and the spoken word.

Going to see a live performance, like going to see a film, is a collective experience, but it differs in one crucial way: the relationship between the audience and the performer is an interactive one. It relies on two-way communication. Essentially, the audience are crucial collaborators in the event. The event requires them to participate, albeit to different degrees, depending on the type of performance. At one end of the spectrum, they may be required to respond by sitting silently in rapt attention occasionally laughing, gasping and crying, and at the other, to actively call out, to vote or even to get up and participate in the action.

Audience response can affect significantly what happens on stage and vice versa. This is what makes live performance so thrilling and so different from night to night. It is why some audiences feel they have to see a show more than once, and why actors love working in the theatre. Performing live is a risk. Actors get a 'buzz' from it. It is why they talk about having 'good' and 'bad' nights.

A writer who is frustrated and made anxious by the variables in live performance should not write for the stage; they should write novels instead.

When you go to the theatre, a contract is made between the audience and the actors. The deal is that the actors give to the audience and the audience show their appreciation. The more audience appreciation, the more actors will play it. Have you ever noticed, at the beginning of a show, how quickly an audience wants to announce its presence to the performers? It is often prepared to laugh at the most unfunny line or piece of 'stage business', just to let the performers know they're there.

Without audience response, the performance is nothing more than a rehearsal.

An audience may be made up of many different constituencies, but the ambition is that they are brought together as one to witness an event in the same ever-changing world as the actors. The lasting impact of the occasion is assured when audience and performers appear to be feeding off each other.

It is for this reason that people who love the theatre talk about the impact of great productions lasting far longer than that of any film.

People say that one of the most significant contributory factors to the force of the impact, is that the event is at a human scale, inclusive and intimate.

THE AUDIENCE

What people are looking for, consciously or not, when they go to a play, is a shared emotional and intellectual experience. Have you ever noticed how, at the start of a performance, the audience is disparate and nervous, and then, as the play progresses, they evolve into a psychological crowd unit, that unconsciously discovers itself? They

A large, diverse audience in the Main Auditorium at Birmingham Rep – a theatre that prides itself on sharing stories for and about its multicultural city.

start acting as one, silent and in awe, smiling and laughing, restless and bored. This experience of knowing that lots of other people share the way you feel and think can be reassuring, thrilling and empowering.

It is a conundrum for playwrights and programmers alike whether they should lead and shape the artistic tastes of their audiences, or whether they should respond to what they already know they want and give it to them. It is best to do a bit of both, and never to underestimate the power of the new and unexpected, to diversify and increase the size of the audience. A writer who wants to make a living must be aware of whatever is currently 'going down well' or 'trending', as well as having an eye to what could be popular in the future. A 'Live Arts' programmer, in order to balance the books, will want to reward loyalty by fulfilling their audience's expectations, but should also be keen to attract new audiences.

New plays are seen as a useful tool in finding new audiences. Playwrights not yet represented by the establishment are seen by some as vital to its survival.

In many arts' institutions, alongside whoever is in charge of choosing what plays should be done, marketing departments are responsible for keeping and finding audiences. 'Marketing' would expect to be consulted about programme choice and audience targets.

Marketing departments speak a different language to most playwrights. They tend to refer to audiences as customers, and they treat them the way any retail business would. They are keen to find out about their habits and their 'wants' through endless satisfaction surveys. Theatre-goers are

Michael Mears in *Life After Scandal* (2007) by Robin Soans. A verbatim play investigating the multimillion-pound industry built on shame, showing how names are blackened and reputations soiled. Premiered at Hampstead Theatre.

regularly asked, in much the same way as on- and offline shoppers, diner-outers, gym attendees, cinema goers, and live music and gallery visitors are asked, to give a free evaluation of their experience, and suggestions as to how that experience might be improved upon. Satisfaction with the play is measured alongside satisfaction with the foyer ambiance, the wine list and whatever else. It would be a full-time job to accede to all their surveys and as far as theatres are concerned, there are too many variables to guarantee a meaningful result. Playwrights should never be over-influenced by the statistical findings of marketing departments and focus groups. They can give you an inflated

sense of your influence or crush your voice and confidence.

The dichotomy for many writers, as to whether they should write for themselves or for a specific audience, is not a useful one. Write for yourself but accept that who you are includes the audience.

Art can follow in the wake of popular taste, but great artists lead far more than they are led.

A COLLABORATIVE AFFAIR

The theatre is a collaborative art form, and a playscript must serve as a template to engage the intelligence, and to inspire the imagination, of a range of artists with different skills (musicians, designers, animators, choreographers and actors) and technicians (lighting, sound, video and digital), all of whom will contribute, to a greater or lesser degree, to the impact of the event.

Historically, however, instructions for the performance have not been paramount in the preparation of playscripts; although there are writers for whom the stage directions are as important, if not more important, than the dialogue. Bernard Shaw's reputation for elaborate and literary stage directions is second to none, and the impact of some of Samuel Beckett's plays rely on his most particular sparse instructions for production.

Most of the time, those members of the public who read playscripts for pleasure have to work hard to imagine their potential in performance. They have to think what the world of the play might look like, what a particular actor might contribute to their role, how might the sound and lighting be used and so on. It is a challenge at the best of times, but when, as in the case of some modern plays, there is no fixed identity to the characters and no linear narrative, it can be particularly daunting. In Sarah Kane's *4.48 Psychosis* (2000), for example, in her evocation of the bipolar experience, the Voices could be doctors, nurses, lovers or whoever… there are no named characters. It is the same in Martin Crimp's play about twentieth-century obsessions *Attempts on her Life* (1997) and Simon Stephen's play *Pornography* (2008), which is a response to the London terrorist attacks of July 2005. Alice Birch's play *Blank* (2019) about what life is like when adults feel absent from it, is sixty scenes long and she challenges the reader or producer to cherry pick the however many scenes and make their own play out of it.

It is much easier to appreciate a play by seeing it in performance, when many of the choices that will have frustrated you whilst reading it have been made.

Depending on the status of the writer in the collaborative production process, a playscript may be seen as something sacrosanct – not a word to be changed without the writer's 'say-so' – or as nothing more than a stimulus text, a text that can be deconstructed and reshaped to reflect the interests and concerns of the group working on it.

SUSPENDING YOUR DISBELIEF

To suspend your disbelief is to accept the stage truth as reality. Stage truth is 'reality edited' – edited to create a particular atmosphere, to tell a certain story, to entertain a one-off audience.

To suspend your disbelief is to know that what you are seeing is pretend reality, but to pretend that you don't know that. By suspending your disbelief, you can immerse yourself in the performance and surrender to the dramatic action, or you can view it objectively, analysing the thesis as the drama unfolds. To suspend your disbelief and engage empathetically with a performance, a second artificial, theatrical world that contains its own truth has to have been created by the production.

Writers, directors, designers, musicians and actors will all use conventions specific to the medium to create this world. For example, if an actor lets the audience know that whenever they are sitting on a particular chair, then they are in the cockpit of an aeroplane, through the repeated and consistent use of the chair in this way, the audience will accept the convention that that's where they are. It is a stage truth.

THE STAGE CONVENTION

A stage convention is a rule that can be set up by the writer, performers and production makers, which the audience understand through repetition to mean a certain thing. It is the consistency of their use that ensures their effectiveness. Commonly, the fewer resources available to a production team, the more they are reliant on establishing conventions to help tell the story. Popular conventions include the use of: slow motion, freeze framing (arresting the action to suggest a passage of time or to shift an audience's focus), the use of soliloquies (a solo speech by an actor that gives an insight into what they are thinking), the use of a narrator or chorus to set the scene or comment on the action and an actor's aside (a direct comment to the audience within a scene). You can make up and establish your own conventions in a performance. Although audiences will want you to be consistent in the way you use them, it is important to remember that by breaking a convention, you can add to the significance of a particular dramatic moment. For example, if you were to take out a real gun in the last scene of a production in which (up until that point) the audience had accepted bits of wood as guns, it is likely to have a far greater impact than if you had been using real guns all along.

WHO IS A PLAYWRIGHT?

The word itself – playwright – is a compound word with no linguistic basis in the word 'writing'. It derives from two Old English words 'plega', meaning brisk movement, and 'writha' meaning worker. The word serves as a reminder that plays are constructed. They are literally wrought.

A playwright is an observer who wants to share their actual and imagined experiences of life with others. A playwright writes stories in dialogue, creating contrasting characters in multiple situations. These impart the playwright's concept – the concept being the idea that governs the play.

The arrangement can be as ingenious as the pattern of a symphony and take as long to structure. Their words can define and determine the parameters of the performance, however abstract the content might be.

Playwrights write for a whole variety of reasons. Some deeply personal – to work through their own anxieties, emotional and ethical – and others, more publicly minded, write to question the times in which they live and to speculate on how the human condition can be improved. They write to ask searching questions, and they hope to change the world, if not globally, then somebody's world, through their incisive observation and comment.

Both types of playwright seek to identify and share the truth about what they have observed and feel about the world.

There are other playwrights who write for the sheer pleasure of hearing actors say their words. Others still are fixated with potential critical and financial success.

Whatever the reason, playwrights should write out of an urge to create. If you don't feel the urge, I would urge you not to do it. Why? Because, for most writers, it is such hard work and the rewards are meagre, unless you are lucky enough to hit the jackpot.

EXERCISES

Exercise 1

Choose a well-known folk or fairy story. Transpose the world of the story to a different time and place, in prose. Assuming your story involves characters, even if some of them are anthropomorphic, *choose whose perspective you are going to tell the story from and why. Write between 500 and 1,000 words. Once you have written it, decide whether what you have written would work better on stage, screen or as audio. Having decided, list your reasons why.*

Exercise 2

Remember what you did on your last birthday. Write the story of that day in prose. Now look around the room that you are in. Consider the objects and who is in the room. Rewrite the story of that day as a play, and stage it quickly, using the resources available to you. Note what conventions you have used to tell your story.

Exercise 3

By adding no more than two lines to each of the following three lines of dialogue, change the nature and atmosphere of the exchange. For example, A and B are madly in love and it's a summer day; or, A and B are about to commit a crime and it is cold and late, and so on.

> A: I thought you'd never get here.
> B: Well, I'm here now.
> C: Let's do it then.

Exercise 4

Practise using a dramatic convention:

THE ASIDE
A convention where the actor talks to the audience without the other characters on stage knowing that's what they're doing.

Write a speech for character who is having to tell another about why they are late for something. While they're giving their reasons to the other character on stage, they are taking time out, in an aside, to explain to the audience the truth.

TIME WARP

Write a speech for a character who is having to tell the story of their life in thirty lines. Choose a phrase like, 'I would still be there' or 'I didn't know any better' that is repeated in the storytelling, and every time it is repeated, the story leaps forward five or ten years.

OBJECT OWNER

Write a speech where Character A is talking to Character B about an object that holds a particular significance for them. The object embodies the spirit of the owner. The reader has to guess who it is.

2
GETTING STARTED

The stressful time is the blank page at the beginning. When you're starting to see things being made flesh, and you're able to respond to that flesh, that's really exciting.

Jack Thorne (playwright, 1974–)

You are alert to the world. You have seen something. You have heard something. You have felt something. You have thought something. Your imagination has been fired and you want to share the experience with others. You have the urge to write a play. Why a play? Because you have a facility with dialogue, and you recently went to the theatre, and the connection between the performers, their characters and the audience gave you an experience like no other. You laughed and you cried. The hairs on the back of your neck stood up. You shivered, tingled and thought differently about the world when you left the performance. You want to change the world. If not for everybody, then for somebody. You want to write a comparable entertainment for anyone who has the good fortune to read it, wants to contribute to the production and experience it live.

Your mind is a smorgasbord of ideas and impressions, but... when you sit down in front of a blank sheet of paper and pick up your pen, or perch in front of a screen and place your fingers on the keyboard, nothing comes out. The impulse to write is there, but you don't know where to start.

You begin to worry that perhaps you don't know enough about whatever it is you want to write about. If your idea is such a good idea, then somebody's probably already done it. If it's been done before, it's bound to have been done better. If it's not been done, there's probably a reason why not. You want to write something innovative and break the rules, but you're not certain what the rules are. Despite thinking that you can write persuasive dialogue, you're not convinced you have the playwriting skills to match 'form' with 'content'. Things go from bad to worse and you start to question what right you have to write about whatever it is you want to write about because it isn't your direct experience, and you don't know where to start your research...

Who has the right to write about whose experience is a thorny debate amongst playwrights, audiences and critics. It will only be resolved when there is equality of opportunity in the art form.

What if what you write isn't perfect? Although you've been told a hundred times 'perfectionism is the death of the imagination and simply a response to trauma that you have got to get over', you can't help the way you feel.

More dark thoughts cross your mind... 'maybe my reasons for writing a play are not altruistic but purely selfish... to show off how clever I am... to have the play produced, yes... but more importantly... published... to see my name in print... I only want to write for posterity, oh... and to earn a lot of money...'. These thoughts are immediately

Richard O'Callaghan as David and Hugh John as Jason in *Our Brother David* (2012) by Anthony Clark. A poignant tale of misplaced love, inspired by Chekov's *Uncle Vanya*. Premiered at Watford Palace Theatre.

superseded by an even darker one. The thought that you are unlikely to find success when the industry is such a lottery; there appears to be no correlation between hard work and originality, and critical and financial success. So, what is the point? You start to despair.

You are having an existential crisis.

You can't see why or how to be a playwright, but the gnawing urge to express yourself in dramatic form won't go away. The way to proceed is to accept that whatever you write, it can always be improved upon. No playwright gets it right first time. Henrik Ibsen, the formidable Norwegian nineteenth-century 'father of realism', tinkered with his verse drama *Peer Gynt* (1867) for most of his life.

Rewriting is where the real writing starts.

WRITER'S BLOCK

All writing is difficult. The most you can hope for is a day when it goes reasonably easily. Plumbers don't get plumber's block, and doctors don't get doctor's block; why should writers be the only profession that gives a special name to the difficulty of working, and then expects sympathy for it?

Philip Pullman (1946–)

Writer's block is a temporary or lasting failure to write. Experienced playwrights, like novice writers, can lose their confidence to write. When you've got it, you procrastinate. No sooner sat at the desk, than you're up making yourself a cup of coffee, listening to music, bingeing on a TV series, going for a walk, catching up on your emails, chatting on the phone, sorting your social life, and doing a little personal administration… anything to distract you from the task in hand. You kid yourself that you are making space for the words to come to you, knowing all along that nothing will work unless you do. 'Writer's block' can make you feel anxious, angry and apathetic, or a combination of all three. It is not that the urge to write isn't there, but you don't really know what to write about and you know only too well that once you get started, the road ahead is long and hard.

If you are one of these writers, none of these displacement activities is actually going to rid you of your spiritual desire to create art, or of the need to find some way to pay the bills.

You've got to get started.

Playwrights will set themselves different challenges to get over 'writers block'. Some will rearrange the furniture in the room where they write. Some will treat themselves to new stationery (yes, it can help) or break their routine and decide to write at a different time of day or night, or to write in long-hand instead of on the computer. Others will think about their ideal audience member and write the story of their play in prose as though they were telling it to them, as a sort of workout of the idea. Some will read a favourite play for inspiration or go to the theatre.

It is important to think about what you would do if you ever had the misfortune of a creative slowdown or lose the ability to write. The novelist and playwright Graham Greene (1904–91) swore by a dream diary, which he consulted when he couldn't see how to progress his work, and sometimes even where to start. Just as a daily diary can help you process your emotions and clarify your thinking, so can a dream diary. Improbable encounters in improbable places can highlight the anxieties you are experiencing, and help you find more creative solutions to everyday problems and situations. The process of thinking about your dreams and asking questions can inspire creativity. Ideas can come from dreams.

A lot of playwrights find 'freewriting' or 'brainstorming' a useful way to get started on a play, or jump-start one when their writing has stalled.

FREEWRITING/ BRAINSTORMING

Night-time is when I brainstorm; last thing, when the family's asleep and I'm alone, I think about the next day's writing and plan a strategy for my assault on the blank page.

Athol Fugard (South African playwright, 1932–)

Freewriting/brainstorming is a technique used to generate creative ideas and solutions. It can be done individually or in groups.

If you are on your own, decide that for the next ten minutes you are going to write, without stopping, the first thing that comes into your head! Start very simply, by writing down a word or a sentence, and let that word or sentence trigger another word… and that sentence or word trigger another… and another… until the page is covered with words and sentences. Treat the task like a game of word association. It's important not to think too hard about what it is you are writing, and don't stop until your time is up.

The hope is that when your page is full and you read over what you have written, your brain will start to make connections between the words and sentences, and the connections will inspire more words and sentences, and then by editing and re-writing what's on the page, ideas, characters, locations, situations, a story (if that's what you want) with themes and a thesis will emerge.

The themes express what your story is really about, and your thesis is your take on your themes.

There is no reason why, at the start of the writing process, you shouldn't let the subconscious lead in this way.

A DEADLINE

Everything is an experiment until it has a deadline. That gives it a destination, context and a reason.

Brian Eno (1942–)

For most writers, the best incentive to start writing is to set themselves, or to be set, a deadline. There is no point, however, in having a deadline if you don't have the discipline to meet it. When the going gets tough, you've got to know you can finish what you have started. Even if writing is something you do in your spare time, you must treat it like a job.

There is no average time it takes a playwright to write a play. Some will think about what they are going to write for a year and write it in three days, and others will take months, perhaps years even, writing for a few hours a day to come up with the goods.

Laura Wade (1977–) took three years to write her most famous play to date, *Posh* (2010). Noel Coward apparently wrote the scenario for *Private Lives* (1930) one evening in hospital while waiting for an operation in Yokohama, and then completed the script a few days later in Singapore. Who knows, however, how long he ruminated over it. The story goes that Alan Ayckbourn, Britain's most produced playwright after Shakespeare, thinks about his plays for a year and then writes them in a matter of days. If you are lucky enough to be commissioned to write a play, you will agree a time with the commissioning organization for the delivery of your first draft. Depending on how busy you are, and the pressures on their programming schedule, this is usually six to nine months.

Decide how you want to plan your time.

If you are not yet in a position to dedicate the whole of your time to writing, because you can't live off what it pays you, it would be advisable to give yourself at least a year to complete a draft of something you are prepared to share with others.

Remember, first impressions last the longest, and it is important not to share your work until it is as good as you can possibly make it. Friends may be more generous, but most theatres will not read a second draft of your play if they have rejected the first one, regardless of the fact that your extensive rewrites may be in response to their notes.

To help you to organize your writing tasks, set yourself a deadline and a series of milestones en route to that date. Milestones are visible indicators of progress. Reaching a milestone on the way to completing your play can give you a real sense of achievement, and help to build and sustain your confidence. Give yourself little treats as you reach each milestone.

TIMETABLE FOR A YEAR

Make use of time, let not advantage slip.

Shakespeare (playwright)

Here is an example of how you might timetable your writing year.

Month One

Concentrate on coming up with an idea or premise. A premise is the proposition – the main purpose for writing your play. For example, the premise for Ibsen's *Ghosts* (1882) is that, 'the sins of the father are visited on the children'. The premise for Caryl Churchill's *Top Girls* (1982) is, 'It takes a lot for women to succeed in a world where equal opportunities are denied them'. The premise for Mike Barlett's play, *Love, Love, Love* (2010) is, 'Baby boomers may have changed the world but at a terrible cost to the next generation'. The premise for Roy William's play, *Sing your Heart Out for the Lads* (2002) is, 'What did it mean to be British in 2000'.

Once you have found your premise, you need to get into 'research-mode' and explore your subject thoroughly. Be careful though, research can be very addictive, especially when we have easy access to so much information online. When new ideas start competing for your attention, don't let yourself be distracted from your original premise. Set yourself some clear research parameters from the outset: What do I need to find out? Where am I going to look for the information? And for how long? Trust the fact that if, further on down the line, your writing leads you to unexpected places (it invariably will), then you can always do more research. This research can have a much tighter focus because it will be informed by what you have already written.

Months Two and Three

From your research, develop your characters, locations and situations. Jot down snippets of dialogue as they come to you. Develop your play's narrative and start to plot the story. A story is everything that happens to all the characters told in chronological order. The plot, however, is this story arranged from a character's, or characters', perspective. Your point of view will be expressed in your decision to tell the story from that perspective. For example, we all know the story of *Little Red Riding Hood*, but if you are an animal rights activist, you might want to tell it from the perspective of the wolf.

Month Four

Work on your scenario. A scenario is a sequence of events that define your plot. In your scenario, identify where a scene is set, who is in it and what happens. (You will probably keep adding details to the scenario as you work through different drafts of your play.) Shuffle your scenes to sort out when and where pieces of information need to be revealed. (To do this, I have known some playwrights cover a wall with 'post-its' describing the bare bones of what goes on in each scene, and then spend hours moving the squares of paper about in order to arrive at an unpredictable sequence of scenes that will maintain the suspense for the viewer and enhance the impact of the playwright's thesis.) Decide when is the best time to start and end a scene, and why. For example, if you're setting a scene at a party, should it be at the beginning, middle or end? Ask yourself what time of year the scene is set. Each time we meet your characters, make sure that we are learning something new about them. Is the space your characters inhabit public or private? What difference does it make? Whose space is it? What motivates your characters to do what they do? How explicit are their intentions? Your scenario can be as detailed or spare as you like, but the more detailed it is, the less likely you are to lose your way when writing the scenes, and the easier it will be to pick up your writing if, for whatever reason, you have had to leave it for a number of hours, days or weeks.

Month Five, Six, Seven and Eight

Settle on your structure. Think more about the circumstances you have created for your characters. Do your characters have a journey? Check that they embody contrasting viewpoints; that they think and operate at different speeds; that they all have wants and obstacles to their wants, which they are challenged to change in the course of the action.

Start to write your dialogue. Collate and connect the snippets of dialogue you have been writing since Month One. Allocate bits of research you have noted in half-formed speeches to various characters. Don't be seduced, however, by the rhetorical, aphoristic brevity of these speeches. If they don't sit easily in the mouths of your characters, and aren't earned in (or applicable to) the situation, leave them in the notebook. Beware of characters speechifying. When this happens, playwrights are often accused of being untrue to their characters and unnecessarily didactic. The playwright is very rarely a character in their own play.

Keep writing until you finish your first draft. Finishing a first draft means getting to the end of the play, knowing full well that the play will need a lot more work.

Month Nine

Do something else for this month. Put your play in a drawer and don't look at it. If you can't stop thinking about it, and are tempted to make changes or have new thoughts about what could happen to enrich your characters and narrative, jot them down in a notebook, not on your script. Keep both script and notebook separate and safe.

Months Ten, Eleven and Twelve

Reread and rewrite, and reread and rewrite, and reread and rewrite, as many times as you need to, concentrating each time on a different aspect of the play. For example: Is the story clear? Do all the characters have a journey? What's happening on stage while the characters are talking? Is the play about anything? At this stage, any piece of writing can always be improved upon. Rewriting requires courage. Rewriting is not simply editing what you have already written. Yes, it can involve correcting your lines, but more often than not it is about altering them in their entirety. Your objective is always to make bad writing good and make good writing better. As the novelist Ernest Hemingway once remarked, 'the only type of writing is rewriting'.

Once you have done all your alterations and corrections, and got your play as good as you can get it, offer the play to somebody else to read. Somebody whom you can trust not to tell you just how 'marvellous' you are, but who can offer you detailed, constructive criticism. Even if your play is good, your outside critic, whilst pointing out what they think you have done well, must be able to point out where it can be improved upon, where there is a lack of clarity, or something is too obvious or beyond credibility.

Although your first response to being criticized may well be to blame the critic and defend what you have done, pay attention to what they say, and think about where you might make improvements. Actors are trained to take notes from the director and think about them before they answer back; playwrights should do the same. The effects of criticism often last a lot longer than praise. If you make the suggested improvements, however, the lasting effects can be far less painful.

Malcom Scates, Geoffrey Freshwater, Avril Clark, Naomi Radcliffe and Jeremy Swift in *The Slight Witch* (2000) by Paul Lucas. A sparkling comedy in which Kirstin, who doesn't feel like a witch, attempts to escape from her family of mystics.

A PUBLIC OR PRIVATE CONVERSATION

Most playwrights get a buzz when their writing occasions a unified response from the audience but there are playwrights who are undoubtedly more interested in having a private conversation between themselves and individual members of the audience – a conversation so private that they may not hear, or wish to hear, the audience's response. Some audiences accuse these writers of being arrogant. They accuse them of wilfully ignoring popular taste, the need for, and power of, empathy and the pleasures of storytelling. They would rather see them banished to the bookshelves of academia. If their work is to be performed at all, let it be done on the Fringe in art clubs and drama schools. They don't want to spend time trying to understand what this work has to offer them. They accuse the playwrights of being 'too experimental', 'too modernist' or 'post-modernist' and even 'anti-theatre'.

'If the only truth this work has to offer is that there is no shared truth to be had from human experience, then that is not a valid response to the human condition', they might protest. But if for some that is the truth of the human condition, then surely, they deserve to be heard.

The problem is that there are examples throughout the history of drama when a playwright's early work has been met with outrage and derision, not because there aren't connections to be made in the writing, but because the audience aren't ready to make them. These playwrights may be talking about things that up until that point haven't been talked about in the theatre, in a way that audiences haven't yet experienced. The form and content of these plays could be pointing us to a truth about the human condition that we have yet to recognize.

Sarah Kane's *Blasted* (1995) was universally misunderstood and condemned by the critics and audiences when it was first produced. They found it utterly bewildering and morally reprehensible. It is now, however, acknowledged to be an insightful, profound and prophetic comment on the connection between physical and psychological violence. It can attract a full house of affluent theatre-goers in a theatre over double the size of the one in which it was first produced.

Often our appreciation of an artist's vision of the world is enhanced by us understanding something of why they are writing the way they are. For example, it is a help to appreciating their work to know that playwrights like Samuel Beckett, Harold Pinter, Arthur Adamov, Caryl Churchill and Martin Crimp sometimes use, disjointed, repetitive, meaningless dialogue, with purposeless action, and plots that defy logic, to comment on, and often criticize, the science of ideology, of judging and reasoning that dominates our technological capitalist age.

Come and Go (1965) by Samuel Beckett elicits a range of different responses from the audience. It is a very short play, only 121 words, that has to be presented with strict regard for the stage directions or the Samuel Beckett Estate won't give the producing company the rights to perform it. The specific nature of the stage directions increases the possibilities of the play's meaning. In the play, three almost identical women, in long, faded, different-coloured coats and wide-brimmed hats that conceal their faces, sit on what may be a bench, but could be a log or a rock. They sit in a pool of light surrounded by darkness. There is no mention of what time it is or where they are. They talk without expression, barely audible. Each in turn leaves the light briefly, moving silently into the darkness, while the other two share an inaudible secret, which causes them to gasp in different ways, and perhaps show pity for the absent one. It appears to be about three women who went to school together, who have now grown old and never married. We hear about the 'then' and we hear about 'the now' and are asked to imagine the time between and speculate on the reasons why. But we are not sure. It ends with the three actors linking hands in a specific way that calls to mind an infinity symbol. Audiences differ in their response to what Beckett was writing about.

That said, they all agree he was writing about something. The play is too finely tuned to be without purpose. Perhaps his purpose was to rescue words from their subservience to a single meaning, which is why he is so particular about how it should be staged. To contextualize the words too specifically would simply diminish their potential to meet and stimulate the imagination of the audience. This play has the power of great abstract art.

Although we can be taught to appreciate abstract art when we know something of the artist's intention, we need to be prepared to look beyond what we already know or recognize. An intangible emotional experience to a piece of theatre that is different for everybody, depending on their state of mind that day, is just as valid as any work that unites and speaks to an audience as one.

The inspiration to write a play can come from any number of sources. It has already been suggested that it can come from a visit to the theatre, but it is more likely to come from an idea you've had, a story you've heard, characters you've encountered, a news article, objects, a location, a poem, a snippet of dialogue, a piece of music or a picture.

Starting with an Idea

> Get a good idea and stay with it. Dog it, and work at it until it's done right.
>
> Walt Disney (1901–1966)

> An idea that is not dangerous is unworthy of being called an idea at all.
>
> Oscar Wilde (1854–1900)

Many writers start their plays with an idea, a thought or a question. They identify themes that appertain to the idea, do their research and come up with a thesis, which is a series of opinions that can be explored and perhaps be proven through the dramatic action.

For example, you may have an idea that you want to write something about the futility and the grotesque spectacle of war. The themes that you are going to consider include violence, patriotism, political ideologies, money, gain and loss, victory, love and death. Your research may lead you to consider a particular conflict, characters or incidents. You devise a narrative that elucidates your themes and expresses what you think and feel about them. You may not be able to answer all the questions that have been provoked by your dramatic action. Don't worry. For some it is the mark of a great playwright if you have presented both sides of a case fairly and are leaving the audience to make up their own minds. Others will crave a more didactic approach.

Robert Hands as Bill Bretherton, Sean Baker as Clement Attlee and Simon Robson as Edward Heath, in *The Schuman Plan* (2006) by Tim Luscombe. Named after the French Foreign Minister who first promulgated the economic unification of Europe, the play moves deftly through the history of post-war Britain.

Remember, that an idea can come from anywhere at any time. Keep a pad, pen, pencil and phone with you wherever you go. Take an active interest in your surroundings. Train your curiosity. Be alert to people you encounter, situations you find yourself in or suddenly imagine. Most importantly, keep abreast of topical events. Look at the world around you and ask yourself questions about why things are the way they are, and how could they be different. Today, for example, what do you think about gender, fake news, climate change, the world pandemic, decolonization, distributionism, renewables, Black Lives Matter and the fallibility of our political institutions?

There is an expectation that a successful writer should be in tune with the zeitgeist. The prolific playwright Mike Bartlett has hit the late twentieth- and early twenty-first-century zeitgeist time and time again with plays like *Artefacts* (2008), *Cock* (2009), *Intervention* (2014), *Love, Love, Love* (2012), *Albion* (2017) and *Snowflake* (2018).

Political Theatre

We need a type of theatre which not only releases the feelings, insights and impulses possible within the particular historical field of human relations in which the action takes place, but employs and encourages those thoughts and feelings which help transform the field itself.

Bertolt Brecht (1898–1956)

There are various types of political play: Agitprop Plays (politically didactic, combative, pop-up plays), Documentary (plays that use pre-existing documentary material for stories about real events and people), Forum Theatre (plays about social injustice in which the audience have the power to stop and influence the narrative), Verbatim Theatre (plays made from the transcription of interviews with real people), plays pertaining to particular political movements (e.g. Marxism, Feminism, LGBTQ) and simply plays that address the political issues of the day to entertain, educate and affect change in society. All these types of play probe the behaviour of human beings as social and political animals.

Some playwrights do this by creating didactic stories peopled by character types that leave the audience in no doubt whose side the writer is on. Their protagonists and antagonists are identified clearly, with the protagonist often unsubtly presented as the mouthpiece for the playwright.

This more didactic, agitational form of political theatre is often criticized for preaching to the converted, but this doesn't negate its purpose. Its purpose being to unite the oppressed against the oppressor by clarifying the issues involved.

This type of theatre is more often than not born out of a political imperative to change the status quo and is starved of resources. As a result, it sometimes challenges established theatrical conventions by being performed in non-traditional spaces – clubs, pubs, the street, workplaces, community centres and found spaces.

Other political playwrights, in the interests of exploring all sides of an argument, will write complex narratives with knotty characters. They are more concerned to create a dialectic through their dialogue, in each scene and play as a whole. The impression given is that they are letting the audience make up their own minds about a subject, but they are, in fact, more often than not, leading them to a particular conclusion.

Being allowed to argue as a means of identifying the truth about the world and how we operate as human beings, is vital to anyone who believes in democracy. It is no coincidence that the idea that power should extend from the governed was born in the same city as the theatre: in Athens in Greece, in the sixth century BC.

The list of playwrights who have explored pressing social and political issues in their plays is extensive and wide-ranging. It would include Sophocles, Aeschylus and Euripides, Shakespeare, Ibsen, Strindberg and Chekhov, Gorky, J. B. Priestley, Henry Arthur Jones, Shaw and Brecht, Arthur Miller, Edward Bond, David Hare and Caryl Churchill, Martin Crimp, Tony Kushner, and Alan Ayckbourn, Joe Penhall, Lucy Prebble,

Richard Bean, Tanika Gupta, James Graham, Mike Bartlett, Lucy Kirkwood, Moira Buffini, Nina Raine, Roy Williams, Gurpreet Bhatti and Zoe Cooper, to name but a few…

For any playwright who wants to engage with, and shape, the contemporary cultural conversation, the theatre serves as a crucible for the truth.

One of the most powerful political plays in recent years was called *The Jungle* (2017) written by Joe Murphy and Joe Roberston. The play immerses audiences in the confusion and chaos of a makeshift city in Calais where thousands of migrants of different nationalities are living side by side. It humanizes migrants, who are often seen as a collective blight on French policies and British consciences. In a series of remarkable scenes based on reality, the play questions why European governments acted with such inhumanity to the idea of so many refugees coming to the continent. Why did the camp at Calais have to be destroyed? It asks if the rich really believe that they can live without 'sharing' indefinitely. How can anyone still propagate free-market capitalism whilst being opposed to the free movement of people? It challenges the assumptions of liberal and conservative audience members alike.

In the United Kingdom, governments of different hues come and go, but the political dramas that have captured audiences' imagination have all had a left-wing bias. Students and critics of the theatre often ask, 'Where are the right-wing playwrights?'. Nick Hynter, ex-artistic director of the National Theatre, mused during a radio interview in 2007 that if he could find a 'mischievous right-wing play', he'd consider producing it. The reason why the vast majority of political plays that are produced have a left-wing bias is that left-wing philosophies focus on inclusivity, intellectual debate and humanitarianism. These philosophies are perhaps more suited to the crucible of the theatre than the politics of the right, that typically support social hierarchies on the basis of natural law, economics and tradition.

It may be difficult to find a play with a right-wing bias but there is no shortage of musicals based

Martin Freeman as King Ethelred in *Silence* (1999) by Moira Buffini, a typical end of the first millennium story involving cross-dressing, hallucinogenic drugs, confused sexuality, alternative religions and apocalyptic dreams.

on right-wing principles of individualism and self-reliance, in which the protagonists shape their own destiny through their own initiative, and their status in life is determined by their own actions and not their place in society.

Just as ideas and themes will suggest characters, situations and a narrative to you, many playwrights start with characters.

Starting with Character

A dramatist who hangs his characters to his plot, instead of hanging his plot to his characters, is guilty of committing a cardinal sin.

John Galsworthy (1867–1933)

There may be no new ideas under the sun. There may be no more than seven basic plots, as the critic Christopher Brooker has suggested in his book of the same title, or only nine stories to tell on stage, as playwright Stephen Jeffreys identifies in his inspiring book *Playwriting* (2019), but what invigorates and distinguishes any story, is character. Characters are people (although in a play, I accept, they can be creatures, beings or things that behave like people). People are individuals. No two people, look, feel, think or behave in exactly the same way, regardless of their social conditioning. Individuals are multi-layered and complex, and getting to know them through what they say and do is the source of infinite fascination for all of us.

The most satisfying plays rely on the growth and evolution of character. Without character to drive your plot, you don't have a story. To be a playwright, you must train yourself to observe and be fascinated by people. You may have seen a face or faces across a crowded room… in a public space… through a rain-drenched pane of glass or in a photograph… a face that, for whatever reasons, excites your curiosity. You may hear them talk and, in your imagination, you create the person behind the face. You speculate on what they might be doing, where they might have come from and where they might be heading. You consider what motivates their actions and the things that stand in the way of them getting what they want. You wonder what strategies they use when real life gets in the way. You consider their likes and dislikes, their politics, their health, their disappointments and aspirations. You do all you can 'to stand inside their shoes'.

Using characters as your starting point, place them in a number of situations and see how they get on, and how much they reveal of themselves. Most characters don't know themselves that well. They are defined by what they do. In every moment in your play they must be under pressure to do something, even if that pressure is to be ignored. They are also defined by what others say about them. Occasionally, a narrator, if they are not identified as a character in the narrative and can be trusted as an impartial witness, will describe a character's characteristics and explain their behaviour to an audience. Using a narrator in this way is more akin to storytelling than playwriting.

Playwrights, like actors, must concentrate on what their characters want, what stands in the way of them getting what they want and what strategies they are going to use to get what they want. Whatever stands in their way, be it a thing or a person, is what creates conflict in a character. Conflict for many playwrights is the essence of drama.

Some playwrights find it useful, when creating characters, to start by placing themselves in the particular situation and imagining how different their characters' reactions would be to their own.

By asking crucial questions about who your characters might be, you get to know who they are. Getting to know your characters well enough to place them anywhere you want to, will require you doing some research. This can be hard work, unless you are writing 'very close to home'. Audiences are sticklers for credibility and consistency, and if, for example, you write a character who is a computer programmer, but you know nothing about coding and how long it takes to write a programme, you'll be found out.

Strive to write well-rounded characters. Well-rounded characters are multi-layered and complex. Their behaviour can be unpredictable and inconsistent but perfectly logical with what we know about them up until that point in your play.

Some playwrights claim that there comes a point in the writing process where their well-rounded characters can take over, and they won't go where they want them to go. They find themselves writing a completely different play from the one they set out to write. Most, however, remain in control of their creations. They manage to place them in credible situations, in which they either succeed or fail, in order to construct a narrative that will reveal their premise. Ibsen spent months of work on his characters before letting them loose in his plays.

It is important to decide who are your protagonists, who are championing a particular cause or idea, and who are the characters actively opposed to them – your antagonists.

All your characters have got to earn their place in your play. To earn their place, they must have a function in your story. Their function will be identified by what they want, and what stands in the way of them getting what they want. In all that they say and do, they must be trying to affect a change in the person they are doing it to, or to the situation. Give to your characters actions and reactions. Make sure these affect a change in them, so that they are different people at the end of the play to how they were at the beginning.

Bearing this in mind, when you start your first play, you may want to start with only a few characters (two to five). It is also worth remembering that the average cast size of play produced in the professional theatre in the UK, before Covid-19 lockdown, was six.

STARTING WITH CHARACTERS IN A DEVISING SITUATION

The world of the characters and their relationships is brought into existence by discussion and a great amount of improvisation – that is, improvising a character. And research into anything and everything that will fill out the authenticity of the character.

Mike Leigh (1943–)

The vast majority of devised plays start with actors and writers working together to build characters through research and improvisation. The hugely successful playwright, screenwriter and director, Mike Leigh, starts by developing characters on a one-to-one basis with the actors.

The actor is asked to create a list of people they know or have known. Through discussion, the characters on the list are shortlisted, on the basis of characteristics that particularly interest the playwright and the actor. A new character is then formed using various characteristics, vocalizations and mannerisms from this chosen bank of people, or even from one individual.

The actors with their individually created separate characters are then brought together in a series of improvisations, from which scenes emerge and a story. The best lines and moments are then honed, scripted and rehearsed. This whole process can take many weeks. What the audience sees is just the tip of the creative iceberg that Leigh and his actors have created.

CHARACTER NAMES

I always start a play by calling the characters A, B, and C.

Harold Pinter

Playwrights can struggle to name their characters. A name has to suit the character. A name has to sound right in the mouth of other characters. Names also have many cultural associations and can help to better place a character. As a result, a character's name can change regularly in the writing process.

The definition of a name – it's worth checking this in a name dictionary or online – can provide you with a thumbnail character sketch, including all kinds of idiosyncratic qualities and attributes, from which you can build a complex, rounded character. The character can be like their name or not like their name. For example, the name Mariam or Mary is often attributed to someone who is gentle and calm, honest, but it could belong to someone who is rough and dishonest. Richard might be an honest strong, handsome ruler or an ugly brute. Subverting expectation and surprising an audience can be a prerequisite for keeping them captivated.

You may, like Harold Pinter, start by calling your characters A, B and C, but it is advisable, unless you have a very good reason not to, to name your characters before asking anybody to read your play. Plays are difficult to read at the best of times and names help distinguish who is saying what to whom. Some writers give their characters a generic name because they don't want you

Two planes fly into the twin towers of the World Trade Centre on 11 September 2001.

to focus on the individual idiosyncrasies of the character but simply describe a generic type, i.e. Woman, Man, Dentist, Doctor and so on.

A Picture Provocation

A good photograph is one that communicates a fact, touches the heart and leaves the viewer a changed person for having seen it. It is, in a word, effective.

Irving Penn (1917–2009)

Today we are bombarded with images. Images of terrible suffering, natural disasters, natural beauty, magnificent achievements, gorgeous people enjoying themselves, country scenes and city life, are coming at us from all types of media. We see so much, that most of the time we see nothing. We are desensitized to the impact of so many visual images. Every now and then, however, our attention is arrested by a photograph or a work of art that resonates with meaning beyond its original context, and demands the world's artists and politicians respond. For example, the terrorist-hijacked planes flying into the twin towers of the World Trade Centre buildings in New York in 2001, or little Alan Kurdi, the dead Syrian refugee child washed up on a beach near Bodrum in 2015. Our initial emotional response will lead us to explore the content of the image and question the context.

Lucy Kirkwood's play, *Chimerica* (2013), would seem to have been inspired, in part, by the famous photograph of the lone Chinese student protestor who confronted a tank in Tiananem Square in 1989. George Kaiser's play *The Raft of*

Medusa (1942), which takes place on a lifeboat adrift in the Atlantic, filled with thirteen children after a passenger liner carrying British evacuees to Canada was torpedoed by German U boats, was inspired by a French painting by Theodore Gericault depicting the aftermath of another real-world naval attack when the desperate crew resorted to cannibalism. Samuel Beckett's play *Waiting for Godot* (1949), was inspired by the early nineteenth-century painting, *Two Men Contemplating the Moon* by Caspar David Frederick. Many musicals have been inspired by works of art: *Fiddler on the Roof* (1964) by Marc Chagall's *The Green Violinist*, or *On the Town* (1949) by *The Fleet's In* by Paul Cadmus.

Starting with a Snippet of Dialogue

> Dialogue is a form of communication in which question and answer continue till a question is left without an answer.
>
> Jiddu Krishnamurti (1895–1986)

You may start with a snippet of dialogue you heard in the street or the workplace, on a bus, train or plane. From that snippet, you again use your imagination, fuelled by research, to invent the character's biography, their dreams and disappointments. You decide on their strengths and weaknesses. You decide on their respective family, friends and enemies. Once you have constructed a plausible character, you can place them in a variety of different situations. These situations will suggest actions and dialogue to you. Think hard enough about what you have written, and a narrative will inevitably emerge.

I was walking to work the other day and I passed two people, a man and woman, in their early thirties I would guess, and the woman said to the man: 'We do the same job. We get the same pay. But he won't answer the phone.' I tried to imagine what sort of job the woman might do and who she might be talking about. In my mind she became the only woman in an estate agent's, who was having to work twice as hard as the men in the office. I thought she might be complaining to a friend who could help her exact her revenge on one particular man – a sexist, lazy incompetent. My mind started inventing all kinds of possible revenge scenarios.

There's a Story to Be Told

Stories are humankind's salvation. People use stories all the time to work out what is happening to them, to reconstruct the past and to imagine the future. So many playwrights, however, find it very hard to write a story, a connected sequence of events that will hold an audience's attention and enlighten us. For a sequence of events to do this, it must be unpredictable yet credible. The events must build on each other. Their effect must be cumulative, with their meanings resonating beyond the literal.

To write a story, it sometimes helps to know the end before you start. If you know the end, you can perhaps work out what is stopping your characters from achieving their goals. And then, how did they manage to overcome what was stopping them reaching their goals? And then, where and when did things start to get in the way (go wrong)?

People say, you will know you have found a good story if you can describe it in two or three succinct sentences. Take the story of *Othello*, for example: Othello finds Desdemona's handkerchief in Cassio's lodging. It has been taken there by Iago for the very purpose of making him jealous. Othello then kills Desdemona and plunges the dagger into his own heart.

Starting with What You Know

When you start writing plays, many teachers, professional directors, producers, dramaturgs and literary managers will encourage you to write about the world you know. They do this because they believe that the audience will find it easier to

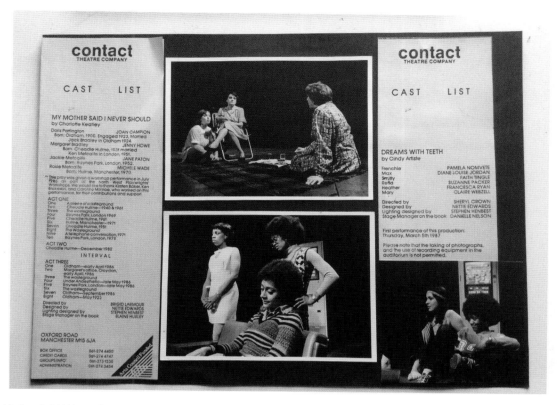

My Mother Said I Never Should (1987) by Charlotte Keatley and *Dreams with Teeth* (1987) by Cindy Artiste, two influential plays by young female writers premiered in repertory at the Contact Theatre in the same season.

suspend their disbelief and appreciate your work if your story's plot, emotional current, characters and dialogue convey authenticity and ring true. They think that this will make it easier for you to write than having to invent from research. They also hope it will stop you writing about things that you think you ought to write about.

Some playwrights and audiences feel that the new writing theatres, in London particularly, have such a prurient interest in what goes on in the lives of people not traditionally represented in the theatre, that they ignore writers with vivid imaginations who are hungry to experiment with theatrical form.

Writing truthfully is about being able to persuade people that what you are writing about has actually happened, is happening or could happen. An imagined sequence of events can equally well present as truth if the cause and effect of the action is credible in the spectator's imagination. Dennis Kelly's brilliant play *Taking Care of Baby* (2007) frustrated critics and audiences by using what they perceived to be a documentary dramatic form, interweaving fiction with reality, to present a lie that pointed out truths about media, political spin and verbatim theatre.

When and Where Do You Write Best and for How Long?

I have learned already never to empty the well of my writing, but always to stop when there was still something there in the deep part of the well, and let it refill at night from the springs that fed it.

Ernest Hemingway (1899–1961)

Caroline Faber and Kate Fleetwood in *Tender* (2001) by Abi Morgan. An acerbic and poignant play that takes a scalpel to modern love and friendship.

This is up to you – in private, in your own work space, in a public space like a library or café, listening to music or in deadly silence, or in a variety of spaces, depending on where you are in the process.

Despite it having been proven, by some scientists, that the optimum time to write is after sleep when the area of the brain that is linked to creativity is most active (e.g. first thing in the morning), there are others who will argue that the best time to write is at night when you are tired and the critical part of your brain doesn't impede progress. You will get to know what time works best for you. Whatever time that might be, it is advisable to keep it regular. Set yourself a start and a finish time. Before you stop, however, always take a few minutes to jot down what you think is going to happen next, so that you don't find yourself reading over and tinkering with all that you have already written, before progressing with the next bit.

Set yourself a word target for each day: if you exceed it, all well and good; if you don't, keep going until you do, or admit defeat and increase the next day's target. Take regular breaks while you are writing and give yourself little rewards as you hit your milestones, e.g. completing a scene. Abi Morgan, who is better known for her television and film work than her plays for the theatre, claims that she works best between nine in the morning and seven at night, at a desk festooned with paper and chocolate.

Formatting Your Text

It is crucial that the script is easy to read and that the margins are big enough to accommodate a reader's notes. Specialist playwriting software, like Final Draft, is available at a price, but a good free package designed for screenwriting, but which works perfectly well for playscripts, is CeltX Microsoft word, or the equivalent is absolutely fine. Your choice of font doesn't matter as long as it's clear. The colour, black. The size 12 or 14. Act or Scene titles should be in bold or underlined or both. It is obviously crucial to attribute lines to specific characters and their names should be in uppercase and in bold, and be set either on the left level with the dialogue or centred above it. Don't forget to number your pages at the bottom or top, on the right-hand side or in the centre. Leave a single line space between a character's lines of continuous

BARBIE'S HEAD

by

A Clark

21/8/16

Agent:
Cathy King
Independent Talent
02076366565

A title page.

CHARACTERS:

Chandra (20s)

Diaba (20s)

Cindy (late 20s)

Chafia (30s)

Aaina (30s)

Tabby (20s)

SETTINGS

2016

A bedsit.
Board Room of an Independent Producing Company 'Fit'
Room in a Flat in Raqqa
In the street in Raqqa
A place in the Syrian desert.

A character list.

speech, and a double line between the speech of one character and the next, or a stage direction. Playwrights sometimes use many more than one or two line spacing as a way of indicating a pause or beat in the dialogue. There are a whole range of signs used by contemporary playwrights to suggest a character's speed of thought and the pace of their delivery, which you may want to incorporate in your script. Or you may want to invent your own. Make sure you define what these are on page 1.

The title page needs only to display the title of your play, your name, the date of the draft, but not what draft it is, and your contact details or those

1

CINDY's small bed-sitting room. CINDY is packing a large
suitcase with personal belongings, including lots of
lingerie. She's having difficulty closing her case when she
suddenly stops. She puts on her music: 'Aqua's Barbie's
World'. She turns out the main light and the room is now lit
by a string of her fairy lights. She starts to dance. She
spins and dances and as the music grows louder, if the
production can afford it both playing space and auditorium
are now twinkling with hundreds of fairy lights.

There is a knock at the door. She doesn't hear it. The
knocking gets louder. She turns down the music. The fairy
lights return to the string in her room.

                  CINDY
          Coming!

2

A Meeting Room of an independent producing company called
'FIT' On one side of the table. CHAFIA, AAINA, and TABBY,
eying the refreshments, Florentine biscuits ,hot and cold
drinks, fresh fruit etc.,. The air conditioning could be
quieter.

                  TABBY
          'Fit' wouldn't have asked us if we
          weren't the best.

                  AAINA
          One of the best, Tabby.

                  CHAFIA
          We need to appear confident.

                  AAINA
          Without being pushy or arrogant.

                  TABBY
          Where are they?

                  CHAFIA
          One of the best of a small group
          of distinctive documentary makers.

                  TABBY
          With a female focus.

                  CHAFIA
          We're good at what we do.

A first page.

of your agent. The title should be in capitals and underlined. It should not be the first numbered page of your play – that should be the first page of the play. Always make sure to number your pages and to date your drafts.

The page after the title page gives the reader some idea of the resources a show might need. A character list is always useful. Only give as much detail in your character descriptions as is essential for the action of your story to be understood. Name, age and gender (if it is not obvious from the name) should be sufficient. Sometimes it is useful to suggest the relationship between the characters, especially if you are writing a family saga.

Any notes on the timeline and setting should also be kept to a minimum.

Don't give a synopsis of your play on this page. A synopsis belongs to the back cover of the published edition.

Don't litter your play with pictures, or include internet links to clips to illustrate 'what you mean' by a stage direction.

EXERCISES

Exercise 1 How to Find a Play in a 'Brainstorm'

- *Set yourself an alarm in 10min.*
- *Choose a verb, e.g. to cry.*
- *Free associate from the verb, other words and sentences, e.g. crying behind a dirty door – of an old house – a baby – whose baby? – person in a dirty dressing gown – depressed – apocalyptic anxiety – pads about on a dirty floor – greasy tiles – nappy stench – baby clothes – her baby? – a pile of ironing – scalded – smoke alarm – burns – a visitor – 'You don't think I'm a good mother, do you?' – mother – sister – older – smarter – has come to help – how to be kind in a cruel world – comfort – pizza –*

cheese onion – birthday party – night – late – out of order – playing the fool – fiancé – wrong person – betrayal, etc.
- *Read over what you have written and see if a theme or theme emerges, e.g. mothering/care, sisters, cruelty vs kindness, betrayal, mental health, etc.*
- *Identify characters suggested by your themes, e.g. baby, mother, mother's sister, fiancé, guests.*
- *Give your characters names.*
- *Using what you have already discovered, and mindful of the subject you are writing about, start to place the characters in situations. Identify the relationships between them, their individual 'wants and needs' and the obstacles that stand in the way of them getting what they want. As you connect the characters, a narrative starts to present itself. One that will ultimately reveal your themes. For example: A young woman lives with her baby in a rural town. She's called Scarlett. Scarlett is suffering from terrible thought intrusions, which could be brought on by post-natal depression or apocalyptic anxiety. Her older sister, Anita, comes to visit her, allegedly to help, but really to accuse her, Scarlett, of seducing her fiancé, Robert. It transpires that she has found out that the father of her sister's child is his. As far as Scarlett is concerned, Anita has got the wrong end of the stick.*

Exercise 2 Unblock Yourself

1. *Get a book, and make a note of how many pages it's got.*
2. *Get a sheet of A2 or A3 paper.*
3. *In the centre of the paper draw a circle (about the size of your fist), and in the centre of it note down one word that sums up what you are going to write about, e.g. love or war.*

4. *Draw four spokes from your centre circle, a quarter of the way towards the edge of the paper.*

5. *Think of a number between say twenty and the total number of pages in the book. Open the book at that page and think of another number between one and ten. Count down that number of lines and find the first noun (or one that appeals to you) on that line. Write the word on one of the spokes. Repeat this task until all the spokes have a word on them.*

6. *Now draw four prongs from each of your four spokes, and write down one word on each of the twelve prongs that are inspired by the word on the spoke. Do this rapidly. As fast as you would if you were playing a game of word association.*

7. *Write sixteen sentences linking the words on your prongs and spokes to your idea/problem in the centre of the sheet of paper.*

The chances are that once you have completed this exercise you will have some new insights into original idea, and you will be thinking differently about it. With any luck, you will have unblocked yourself.

Exercise 3 Plot a Story

1. *Write the story of a well-known fairy tale down on a side of A4.*

2. *Identify from whose perspective you have told the story.*

3. *Assuming it is that of a character within the story, choose to tell the same story from a different character's perspective.*

Exercise 4 The Playwright's Clock

The Playwright's Clock is a diagram of a timetable that can help you to organize information and better understand the relationship between tasks.

Get a large sheet of paper and draw a big circle on it. Then divide the circle into twelve segments to represent the months of the year. In the centre of the circle, draw a little circle, like the bull's eye on a dart board, and write the working title of your play inside it. Then fill in the segments with the milestones you intend to reach each month.

Exercise 5 A Scenario

Write the scenario for a scene.

Decide when and where the scene takes place. Does it take place in real time? What happens? Who is involved? What are they doing? How are the characters affected by what happens?

Exercise 6 Developing an Idea

This exercise will help you to come up with different ways of thinking about your original idea. Get yourself a large piece of paper (A3) and draw a fist-sized circle in the middle of it. Write your idea in the centre of the circle. Then draw four branches off the circle and write four words associated with your idea. Draw four more branches off each of these words and, at the end of each branch, write another word associated with the word at the end of the branch. Then write up to sixteen different sentences that each combine the four words on each branch: the word on the outer branch, the inner branch, the first word and the topic.

Having done this, the chances are you will have come up with new ways of considering your original idea.

Exercise 7 A Snippet of Dialogue

Record a random snippet (1 to 1½ min of dialogue). Listen to it a few times and imagine who owns the words and what they might be talking about. Let the words suggest a conversation between two to five people. Imagine what the relationship is between your characters and what they are doing. Write one short three-page scene that has a definite ending.

Exercise 8 A Picture Provocation

Choose a figurative picture, photographic or painted, with a number of characters in it. Think about who the characters might be and the relationship between them. Think about what happened before the picture was taken, what happened when it was taken and what happened after. Write three short scenes: the preceding scene, the scene in the picture and the scene after.

Exercise 9 Building a Character

Concentrating on your characters' physiology, their sociology and psychology, answer the following questions:

- *Physiology:*
  - *What do they look like?*
  - *What race are they?*
  - *How do they describe their sexual orientation?*
  - *How old are they?*
  - *Do they have any physical peculiarities?*
  - *How do they move? Sit?*
  - *Do they sleep? For how long?*

- *Sociology:*
  - *What is their home life?*
  - *Where do they fit in the family?*
  - *Where do they live?*
  - *What class are they?*
  - *Where did they go to school?*
  - *Where do they work?*
  - *What do they do?*
  - *Are they religious?*

- *What are their politics?*
- *What are their hobbies?*

- *Pyschology:*
  - *How do they think?*
  - *Are they intuitive?*
  - *Are they introverted? Extroverted?*
  - *What's their temperament? Aggressive? Loving? Anxious? Relaxed? Neurotic? Evil? Godly? Easy going? Pessimistic? Optimistic?*
  - *What gives them pleasure? How do they find gratification?*
  - *How do they maintain their self-esteem?*
  - *Do they have complexes? Obsessions? Inhibitions? Superstitions? Phobias?*
  - *Have they been affected by trauma and, if so, how?*

If the answers to these questions haven't given you a strong sense of who your characters are, you may want to ask other types of questions – questions that stimulate your imagination in a completely different way. For example: What do they dream about? What's their favourite colour, food, season, time of day? What do they have in their pockets? Don't get too bogged down with the reasons why.

Exercise 10 The Event Trigger

Think of five significant moments in your life time when you were affected by outside events e.g. Covid-19, the Black Lives Matter protests, a first encounter with death, sex, birth, love, a popular song, a sporting event, a terrorist attack.

Choose three characters suggested by the event. Write a short scene (three pages) for all three, contrasting their reactions to the event with your own. Decide where they are, whose space it is and what are they doing in that space. Make sure your scene has an ending.

Exercise 11 What's in a Name?

Chose three names from a name dictionary. Check what they mean. Build a character, with their dominant characteristics having been suggested by their name, e.g. the name Keen is a British name and means wise and proud, Damilola is an African name and means blessed with wealth, Tabitha is a Hebrew name and means a gazelle.

Try inventing a name – a unisex name that directs you to write in a non-gender specific way, or the name for a robot.

3
THE IMPORTANCE OF STRUCTURE

I personally would like to bring a tortoise onto the stage, turn it into a racehorse, then into a hat, a song, a dragoon and a fountain of water. One can dare anything in the theatre and it is the place where one dares the least.

Eugene Ionesco (1909–1994)

A number of factors will contribute to making your writing dramatic. Some have already been mentioned like the strength of your idea, the definition of your characters and the authenticity and distillation of your dialogue. It will be the way you bridge the gap between your intuitive response to stage practice and your knowledge of playwriting theory that will determine the structure for your play and ensure its impact.

In the same way that a maquette can help the sculptor visualize their finished work, help sort out what materials to use and how to set about making their piece, so a playwright who plans their play in advance can save themselves an enormous amount of time and stress. If, before you start your play, you can decide on your themes, your story and from whose point of view you are going to tell it; if you can write a scenario to work out what needs to happen, when, where and how; then you will find the job of completing a first draft a lot easier, than having to make it up as you go along. Completing a first draft means to arrive at a possible ending.

Of course, devising a linear narrative, with actions driven by causality, with characters on clear journeys, is not the only structure available to you. Your structure could be determined by something completely different. For example, you may want to write a series of short scenes that are an expression of an emotional response to something you feel strongly about that aren't linked by a narrative. If so, you will have to find your own imaginative way of holding our attention, by varying the pace and spectacle to deliver your content.

The real work of writing a play lies in its construction. A play has nothing like as many words as a novel or a biography but it can take as long to write. The effort is in the thinking and the organizing. If you write five pages of dialogue a day, you can have written a full-length play in sixteen days. You could write maybe ten plays a year, maybe more… but no playwright does this.

There are many playwrights, particularly first-time writers, who will start on the journey of writing a play without knowing where they are heading. If you are one of these, as long as you have got the confidence and self-discipline to keep writing until you have completed a first draft, that's fine. Reaching the end will then give you a chance to look back and check whether your play is doing what you want it to. Is your story clear? Is there enough going on? Do your characters change as a result of what they instigate and what happens to them?

Of course, you can start by not knowing where you are going and stop en route to plan the rest of the journey.

STRUCTURE THROUGH THE AGES

Throughout history, theories of dramatic structure have evolved to reflect the sensibilities of the age and their country of origin. European ideas about dramatic structure, which are the main concern of this book, have had a significant global influence. That is not to say that writers of different ethnicities have not brought different sensibilities and approaches to a European model, and that European writers haven't appropriated dramatic forms from other cultures. European dramatic structure has its roots in Ancient Greek theatre (particularly Tragedy), Roman theatre and Medieval folk theatre.

A typical Greek tragedy would begin with a prologue, in which one or two actors would introduce the topic of the play. This would be followed by the Chorus – a homogeneous, non-individualized group of masked performers who would provide background information on the story, summarize the themes and comment on the dramatic action. They would then stay on stage for the duration of the play and would, from time to time, interact with the actors. The story would unfold in a series of episodes, interspersed by choral interludes. The playwright Aeschylus (525–456BC), who it is believed wrote up to ninety plays, only seven of which survive, including *The Oresteia*, *The Suppliants* and *Prometheus Bound*, is credited with introducing the idea of conflict into the drama by having more than one actor interact with the Chorus. Then Sophocles (496–406BC), who it is believed wrote over 120 plays, whose notable works include *Oedipus Rex*, *Antigone* and

Greek and Roman playwrights.

Electra, introduced a third actor, which increased the complexity of the story. He also extended the audience's empathy for his characters by making them more human. After Sophocles, a playwright called Euripides (485–406BC), who wrote as many plays as Aeschylus, nineteen of which have survived, including the *Medea*, *The Bacchae* and *The Trojan Women*, found less and less use for the Chorus, as he strove for a new psychological realism in his work. He directly referred to contemporary events in his work, and is noted for writing fierce and treacherous heroines.

Roman theatre ranged from street performances to the situational comedies of Plautus (254–184BC) and the gory tragedies of Seneca (AD4–65). Unlike the Greek tragedians, Seneca was preoccupied with dramatizing the central causes of his characters' emotional conflicts, and he explored the inner workings of their minds through soliloquies. The plays are renowned for their bloodthirsty descriptions and had a huge influence on Elizabethan and Jacobean drama. In his plays, the gods rarely appear but they are full of ghosts and witches. His most popular plays include *Medea*, *Thyestes* and *Phaedra*. Plautus, who was as prolific a dramatist as Sophocles, adapted Greek comedies but removed the Chorus as the means of separating the action into distinct episodes. The comedies were set in the street or in the house of the main characters, and were heavy on plot. The plays themselves have not stood the test of time but the stock characters in them were later to emerge in various guises in the plays of any number of European playwrights, including Goldoni (1707–1793), Moliére (1622–1673), Pirandello (1867–1936) and, of course, Shakespeare (1564–1616).

Medieval theatre refers to a variety of genres, including liturgical drama called mystery plays (named after the Latin word for 'occupation', as they were performed by artisan guilds). Mystery plays were synonymous with miracle plays. Both were morality plays covering just about every story in the Bible. There were also other forms of secular farces and masques performed for a largely illiterate audience.

In the face of a new world order, known as the Renaissance (fourteenth to seventeenth centuries), which saw individuals taking responsibility for their own actions and challenging the predominance

of fate, religion and social law, Shakespeare and his contemporaries broke with classical Greek, Roman and Medieval theatre traditions. They wrote characters who were multifaceted, particularly Shakespeare (1564–1616). Shakespeare's characters are preoccupied with the struggle between their personal ambitions and the right thing to do for society, and the world at large. Structurally, he extended his stories and started them at the earliest possible point. He developed subplots, and often alternated between comic and tragic scenes. He experimented with language, mixing verse and prose, frequently – but not always – to distinguish different classes of character and to heighten the emotional impact of certain scenes. In his later plays he used prose more frequently as he sought, with greater realistic accuracy, to 'hold a mirror up to nature'.

For the next two hundred years, writers, as they have always done, challenged the accepted way of doing things, by extending old ideas and coming up with new ones. Popular genres included revenge tragedy, Restoration comedy, city comedy, pantomime and melodrama – all had their time.

In the nineteenth century, 'realism', which was part of a broader theatrical movement that included 'naturalism' and 'social realism', became the dominant theatrical aesthetic and remains so today. Writers like Chekhov (1860–1904), Gorky (1868–1936), Strindberg (1849–1912), Ibsen (1828–1906), Hauptman (1899–1936), Henry Arthur Jones (1851–1929) and Galsworthy (1867–1933) sought to recreate a facsimile of real life on stage. Narratives, typically, were psychologically driven and included day-to-day, ordinary scenarios. Narrative action moved forward in time, and supernatural presences (gods, ghosts, fantastic phenomena) were out.

Throughout the twentieth century, but particularly in the early half, in response to, or alongside, a plethora of movements in the visual arts that sought to encapsulate the alienating experience of rampant capitalism, corrosive and fanatical political idealism and war, playwrights experimented wildly with theatrical form. Playwrights like W. B Yeats (1865–1939) and Antonin Artaud (1896–1948) pushed against what was happening, by retreating to writing ritualistic plays, without direct statement, relying on the rhythm of language and disconnected images, in search of spontaneity that would touch and feed the subconscious. They, like the symbolists Hugo von Hofmannsthal (1874–1929), Maurice Maeterlinck (1862–1949) and Leonid Andreyev (1871–1919), wanted to see a theatre of enchantment and ecstasy. The futurist dramatists spurned sterile realism and the traditional, popular psychological subject matter for something more visceral and intellectual. The Dadaists, and surrealist dramatists like Lorca (1898–1936), Picasso (1881–1973), Apollinaire (1880–1918) and Cocteau (1889–1963), wanted rid of any trappings of illusion and realism. The stage was to create reality in its own terms.

Expressionism was the most significant avant-garde theatre of this period. Expressionist playwrights, like other modernists, rejected the trappings of realistic theatre. They sought to explore the experience of the human soul and brain in the midst of an increasingly violent and mechanistic world. They distorted and abstracted language and stage settings to portray and elicit from their audiences a vital, subjective, emotional and intellectual response. Leading exponents of expressionist theatre included Ernst Toller (1893–1939), Elmer Rice (1892–1967), Sophie Treadwell (1885–1970), Georg Kaiser (1878–1945) and Bertolt Brecht (1898–1956). Arthur Miller (1915–2005), Tennessee Williams (1911–83) and Eugene O'Neill (1888–1953) all had a go at writing an expressionist play, in an attempt to get at the truth of the human condition.

Modernism is a movement that incorporates all formal experimentation in the theatre that departs from the classical traditions of playwriting practised since the Renaissance. It is ongoing in its pursuit of the truth of existence. Famous modernist playwrights, other than those already mentioned, would include Frank Wedekind (1864–1918), Tom Stoppard (1937–) and T. S Eliot (1888–1965), and the so-called Absurdists (a name coined by the academic Martin Esslin in his book *The Theatre of the Absurd* to define the work of a number of different playwrights whose plays emphasized the absurdity of the human condition) – Samuel Beckett (1906–1989), Eugene Ionesco (1909–94) and Fernando Arrabel (1932–).

Post-modernist playwrights don't see the need to reveal universal truths about humankind in their work. Such truths don't exist anymore, if they ever did. They doubt that a single ideology will ever allow the human race to progress. Therefore, no form or content is better or worse than any other. They are excited by inconsistency and eclecticism. They are happy to combine many styles of writing in what they write. Post-modern plays are complex and contradictory, and even for adventurous theatre-goers are an acquired taste.

In the past half century, post-modernist playwrights like Caryl Churchill, Howard Barker, Edward Bond, Martin Crimp, Sarah Kane, Dennis Kelly, Lucy Kirkwood, Moira Buffini, Tim Crouch, Alice Birch, Antony Neilson and Alistair McDowell have all experimented with dramatic form and written stylistically bold plays, in order to explore the diverse, fractured and often overwhelming nature of contemporary experience. Knowledge of the modern world is so extensive that it requires complex expression. So, it seems, every contemporary writer must be allowed to make their own rules.

Many of these would argue, however, that they have not dispensed with the old rules and conventions, just for the sake of it. In the same way that painters are encouraged not to use the practice of abstract painting as an excuse to neglect such vital areas as drawing, perspective, plasticity, colour theory, composition, shade and three-dimensionality, playwrights need to know something of the theory of dramatic writing, how to tell a story, how to create suspense and atmosphere, and to evolve character through dialogue, before breaking with whatever is the norm.

Some critics and more conservative audiences claim that the desire to break the norm is so strong amongst some contemporary playwrights that they can appear to be without skill. They accuse these playwrights of being gimmicky, trying something different just for the sake of trying something different and they blame them for turning audiences away from serious theatre. Ground-breaking playwrights accept the responsibility of the artist to be true to themselves and their audience.

The influence on contemporary playwrights of Hans Thies Lehmann's book *Post Dramatic Theatre* (2006), cannot be underestimated. In it, Lehmann (1944–) summarizes a number of tendencies and stylistic traits of the avant-garde theatre since the 1960s. He argues against the hierarchical dominance of the playwright in Western theatre, suggesting that equal, if not more, attention is now being paid, and should continue to be paid, to the contribution made by other significant production makers, such as the director, performers, designers, musicians and dancers.

If playwrights, who have traditionally set the template and provided a consistency of voice for the production, are no longer the person to whom the rest of the team defer, that does not relieve them of their responsibility. Many playwrights are happy for their texts to serve as stimulus texts for production, and have adapted their writing process to respond to the input from other collaborators. They will often work as dramaturgs responsible for researching, inventing, developing and editing dialogue to express the collective thesis through narrative.

Matching the form to the content is still crucial to the job of any playwright.

THE CONVENTIONAL STRUCTURE OF DRAMA IN THE WEST

Aristotle (384–322BC)

Aristotle was a biologist and philosopher, and he applied his scientific approach and knowledge to

Plato and Aristotle by Raphael.

theatre, amongst other things. He realized that narrative couldn't exist without structure and so set about trying to understand how dramatic stories were structured to engage audiences.

Plato (428–347BC), before Aristotle, another philosopher and Aristotle's teacher, had associated dramatic art with 'mimesis' and the imitation of reality that claimed to be the truth. Aristotle took this one stage further, by suggesting that the dramatic arts were not simply a representation of reality, but a condensing of reality that identified the probability of something happening, and the necessity for it to happen. So, in essence, we experience two realities when we watch a play – an aesthetic reality and an empirical reality. The aesthetic reality has its foundations in the empirical reality, but it lives in the imagination. By understanding the conventions of the art form, by reading the signs and using our imaginations, we are able to suspend our disbelief and appreciate what we are watching.

In the fragments we have of his book *The Poetics*, Aristotle identified six vital components as being necessary in a good drama: plot, character, diction, thought, spectacle and melody.

The plot, for Aristotle, worked in a particular way: it had to have a logical line of 'action'. By 'action' Aristotle didn't mean a physical action, but a character's internal psychological need, their 'want' that drove them forward. 'Action' is what a character wants. The action had to have a beginning, middle and end, and it had to be of a certain 'magnitude'. There is a lot of discussion about what he actually meant by magnitude. It is generally understood to mean not too small to pass unnoticed, and not too big and complicated to be impossible to understand and remember.

Here are some terms that help to explain how Aristotle observed dramatic structure working:

- Hamartia – refers to the protagonist's error of judgement, which leads to their eventual downfall. This is more redeemable than 'hubris' because it is connected to human 'action'.
- Hubris – refers to an inherent flaw in the central character (i.e. excessive pride).
- Peripeteia – refers to a reversal of expectation, circumstance or fortune.
- Anagnorisis – refers to the acquisition of self-knowledge. This usually happens when the protagonist is confronted with 'peripeteia'.
- Catharsis – refers to the feeling with which the audience are left, having witnessed the drama. In response to the resolution of the plot, they are left purged of any feelings of anxiety, pity and fear that they may have had whilst watching the drama.

A dramatic story structure, Aristotle observed, contains five crucial points:

1. Exposition (placing the setting, and meeting the characters)
2. Complication
3. Climax
4. Consequence
5. Resolution

SOME FAMILIAR STRUCTURES

To enable playwrights to hit these points, the Roman theorist Horace (65–8BC) wrote in his book *The Art of Poetry* a series of rules for a five-act structure. He saw this structure as the only legitimate one for drama. The five-act structure dominated Western theatrical practice throughout the sixteenth, seventeenth and eighteenth centuries. Horace's interpretations of Aristotle's observations, however, were regularly misinterpreted. One of these was to do with the restrictions of time and location placed on the drama, which, it could be argued, thwarted theatrical innovation for many years.

In the late eighteenth century, however, playwrights had started to experiment with three acts as being a more appropriate structure for their writing, because stories really only had three movements – a beginning, a middle and an end. Each act has a role to play in setting up what follows. Sequences within these stories, and sequences within sequences, repeat the same pattern – a pattern that reflects our journey through life. By the nineteenth century, the rules associated with the five-act structure were abandoned in favour of three acts. Some have suggested that it was actually the advent of screenwriting, which considered Horace's rules to be antithetical to the aesthetics of the new medium, that finally saw off the five-act structure. In many ways, the one-act, two-act, four-act and five-act plays are all variations of the three-act structure.

The One-Act Play

A one-act play is to the three-act play what the short story is to the novel. It will be shorter, lasting somewhere between forty minutes and an hour and fifteen minutes. The action will usually be confined to one setting and take place in real time, though not always. A one-act play may consist of scenes but is more likely to be one continuous scene. Two or more one-act plays are sometimes presented as an evening's entertainment. These are called a double bill or triple bill. Famous one-act plays would include *Krapp's Last Tape* by Samuel Beckett (1906–1989), *The Goat or Who is Sylvie?* by Edward Albee (1928–2016), *The Bear* and *The Proposal* by Anton Chekhov (1806–1904), and many classical Greek dramas. In length, the script should be anywhere between thirty-five and fifty pages.

The Two-Act Play

The internal narrative structure of a two-act play and a three-act play won't look that different. Usually, the only difference will be where the playwright, the producer or director has chosen to stop the action for an interval. For the past nearly one hundred years, there seems to have been a requirement on the part of the audience that they should have at least one opportunity during the performance to get up, stretch their legs, go to the loo, have a drink and check their phone. Theatre managements will often insist on

there being an interval in order to boost their bar profits, which in some cases help to subsidize the costs of the production or the theatre's overheads. In order to ensure that an audience returns to their seats after the break, many playwrights have learned to build the action to a significant climax by the end of the first act. At the interval, you want the audience to go into the foyer desperate to share their experience of what they have just seen with their colleagues and to speculate on what might happen next. Many playwrights use the interval between Act One and Act Two to suggest a passage of time or to mark a change of location. The two-act play is the standard form of playwriting these days, though it won't necessarily be described as a two-act play. A play in two parts is a more familiar descriptor. In length, your script should be anywhere between 70 and 100 pages.

The Three-Act Play

The three-act play is a simplified version of the five- and four-act structure that preceded it. In Act One, the major characters of the drama are

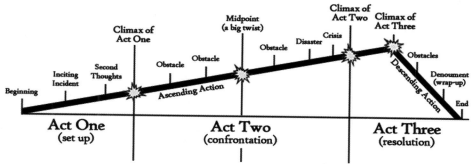

The three-act play structure.

introduced and the differences between them set up. You should also establish what world they are in. The trick with Act One is to start it at a point where there is already conflict between the characters, so that the audience start asking questions immediately about what is going on and why. Open with a 'hook' – something that is said or done, that lures and catches an audience's attention like a fish is lured and caught by a fisherman's hook. By the end of Act One, we should be able to identify the protagonist and the antagonist, and feel confident that we understand, if not fully, then we have an idea of, the relationships between all the characters, primary and secondary.

In Act Two, you build the conflicts between the characters. The situation they have either created for themselves or find themselves in has become more difficult. Sometimes this is achieved by introducing us to a bit of a character's backstory that we were not aware of in the previous act, or by introducing us to a new character or major physical event (the outbreak of war, an earthquake). By the end of the act, your protagonist should be either physically or emotionally (or both) in big trouble.

In Act Three, your protagonist finds ways to move on from, or be defeated by, the circumstances they met at the end of Act Two.

Along with what has already been said about the three-act play, each act tends to have a completely different tone. It can be set in a different location and at a different time of day.

The Four-Act Play

In a four-act structure, the second act of a three-act structure is divided in two. The first act still deals with the set-up. The second act now deals with establishing the conflicts between the characters. The third act deals with these conflicts coming to a head – the climax. The fourth act deals with the fallout and the resolution.

Four-Act Structure

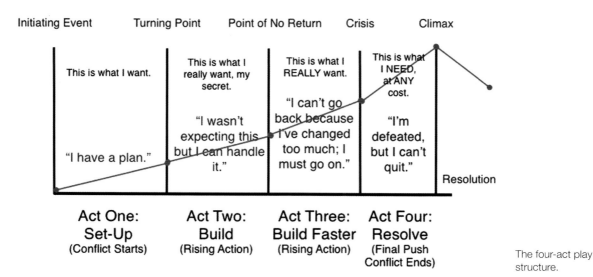

The four-act play structure.

The Five-Act Play

In 1863, the German playwright Gustav Freytag, like Aristotle and Horace before him, identified a five-act structure in any plot.

He had slightly different names for the acts: exposition, rising action, climax, falling action and dénouement. He produced a pyramid to demonstrate this idea, which is known as the Freytag pyramid.

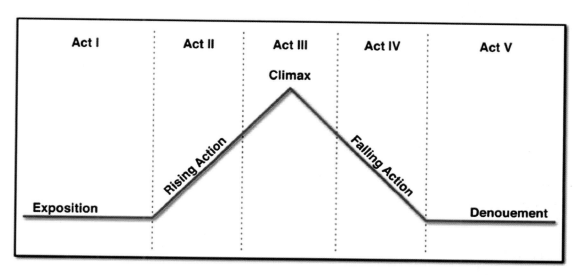

The five-act play structure.

Gustav Freytag (1816–1885). Portrait by Karl Stauffer-Bern.

Freytag's Triangle, a dramatic structural framework developed in the mid-nineteenth century.

The five acts can be broken down as follows:

1. **Exposition.** This is an introduction to the world and the characters of the play. It also contains what is often referred to as the inciting incident. An incident that forces a reaction from the main players in the narrative. For example, if we look at Shakespeare's *Macbeth*. In Act One, we learn about the state of Scotland and who the main players are, with the inciting incident being Macbeth and Banquo meeting the witches on the heath, and their prophecy that Macbeth will be king and Banquo's sons kings ever after.

2. **Rising action.** The narrative develops as the characters are confronted with obstacles that get in the way of them, resolving the situation caused by the inciting incident. Again, looking at *Macbeth*: in Act Two, Macbeth must give in to his ambition, repress his feelings of loyalty for King Duncan, who has recently honoured him and, with the support of Lady Macbeth, commit to killing him. He does so.

3. **Climax.** This is the turning point of the story. This is the midpoint. It is the point of the highest tension. In Act Three, Macbeth has to hide his crime and secure his position as king. He must have Banquo murdered. This he manages, but Banquo's son, Fleance, escapes. When Banquo's ghost appears at a dinner, he is forced to deal with his guilt.

4. **Falling action.** The fallout after the climax. Macbeth visits the witches and they confirm his worst fears in presenting him with three apparitions: one tells him to 'Beware the Thane of Fife, Macduff'; a second reassures him that he need fear 'no man of woman born'; and a third is a line of eight kings all related to Banquo. Macbeth murders Macduff's wife and children while Macdiff is away in England trying to persuade King Malcolm he should come to Scotland and rid the country of the tyrant Macbeth.

5. **Dénouement.** This is the resolution of the story where conflicts are resolved and loose ends tied up. This is the moment of emotional release for the audience – the moment of catharsis. Lady Macbeth goes mad and kills herself. Macbeth is confronted with Macduff and loses the fight when he discovers that he was 'from her womb untimely ripped', and Malcolm leads a victorious army against Macbeth and is crowned King of Scotland.

The length of the acts in a five-act play can vary significantly, as can the length of the scenes within an act.

The Episodic Play

In an episodic play, the action unfolds as a series of episodes, not necessarily in chronological order. The scenes often stand alone, each with their own climax. The plays can cover many locations over many years, typically, including subplots in addition to the main story. Short scenes alternate with longer scenes, public scenes alternate with private, comic scenes alternate with serious scenes. Apart from Shakespeare, other playwrights who use the episodic structure include Johann Goethe (1749–1832) who wrote *Faust* Parts One and Two (1808), Georg Buchner (1813–37) who wrote the enigmatic short play *Woyzeck* (1835), Bertolt Brecht (1898–1956) whose famous plays include, *Mother Courage and Her Children* (1939), *The Life of Galileo* (1943) and *The Caucasian Chalk Circle* (1948), Jean Genet and many contemporary playwrights, particularly those writing for large stages like Tony Kushner *Angels in America* (1991), Moira Buffini *Welcome to Thebes* (2010), Mike Barlett *Earthquakes in London* (2010) and *13* (2011), David Hare *Pravda* (1985), *A Map of the World* (1982), David Edgar *Pentecost* (1995), *Maydays* (1983) and Howard Brenton *The Romans in Britain* (1980), *55 Days* (2012).

Tyrone Huggins, Owen John O'Mahonny, Claude Close, Joan Carol Williams and Ellie Haddington in *Mother Courage and Her Children* (1939) at the Contact Theatre.

A Ten-Minute Play

A simple, short story told in dialogue that lasts no more than ten minutes. A play of this length is very rarely performed on its own but as one of a series of plays in a festival or in an evening showcasing competition entrants. This form is not to be confused with sketch writing. A sketch can last between three and ten minutes, and will have a beginning, a middle and an end, but its primary purpose will be to make people laugh. The characters will invariably be comedy stereotypes and the setting generic.

A Dramaticule

A short or insignificant drama, but not a sketch. The word is how Beckett describes his play *Come and Go* (1966), which is only two pages long.

A Duologue

This is a scene for two characters – a conversation between them that contains both explicit and implicit meaning. It is the foundation of all dramatic writing.

A Monologue

A monologue is a play that is a long speech by one character that tells a story that is usually addressed directly to the audience. If it is to the audience, the character is casting the audience as another character or characters. The same word is also sometimes used to describe an extended speech within a scene.

A Soliloquy

This is a type of monologue but, more specifically, it is conversation that the character is having with themselves.

Free Structure

If you have a new way of seeing and understanding the world, then the structure you choose may match with none of the above.

The pressure to adhere to a particular structure should never get in the way of your particular vision.

ACTS, SCENES AND BEATS

Acts are only convenient ways to divide plays into manageable chunks for writers, their publishers, their readers, directors, designers and actors. Acts can be further divided into scenes, and scenes into beats. A theatrical 'beat' is not a sound effect but a section of text that contains an action, an obstacle and an event.

An action, as we have already identified, is a character's need or want. For dramatic purposes, obstacles are placed in the way of a character's needs. The obstacles can be internal (a physical or psychological disability) or external (social or environmental).

An event describes the outcome of the conflict between the need and the obstacle; the point at which the characters either do or don't get what they want. An event can also be a moment of interruption when something happens that takes over from what has gone before. This inevitably happens when a new character enters the scene.

In published editions of plays published in France and Russia, new scenes often start whenever a character enters or exits. The assumption is made that the character entering with a strong action is always an event, and so is a character leaving, having got as far as they could get with their particular action.

Events are the moments of change in a scene or in an act. The impact of the last beat in any scene or act is usually greater than that of any beat contained within the scene or act up to that point. The event within the final beat of the scene should mark a significant turning point or advance in the narrative of the play as a whole.

Identifying beats in a scene is often a matter of some debate in rehearsal. The interpretation of a scene will depend on where the director and actors decide to mark the beats.

CONFLICT

Dramatic stories, and the themes within them, unfold and are sustained through a series of conflicts. An essential ingredient in most Western drama is conflict. Conflict is the thing that prevents a character getting what they want. The obstacle can be internal or external. An internal conflict is usually a psychological one, or a physical illness. An external conflict is when a character is pitted against fate, against themselves, against another person, against society, against the environment, the supernatural or technology. Conflicts reveal the differences between characters and invariably lead to more conflict. Establishing differences between your characters, however, doesn't automatically lead to conflict. No two individuals, like your characters, should be alike, but they can be united by their common humanity. It is only when the differences between them become more important than what unites them that there is real dramatic conflict. The content of the conflict may not be that important in the great scheme of things, but to hold our attention, what is at stake must be high in the context of the play. More often than not, if your character wants something – what are they are going to have to change to get it? Conflict causes things to change and change is the bedrock of life.

When you start a play, go straight to a moment of conflict and, if you can't get there immediately, get there as fast as you can, and finish the scene as soon as the resolution occurs, or is obvious. This will give your writing momentum. The key to writing a successful scene is to 'arrive late' and 'leave early'.

For centuries, Chinese and Japanese writers have used a plot structure that doesn't rely on conflict. Instead it relies on contrast and exposition to hold the audience's attention. The structure is known as *Kishotenketsu*. No obstacle impedes the progress of the protagonist.

The 6,000 couplets of *The Natyashastra* (500BC) are an ancient Sanskrit treatise on performing arts. They contain the oldest assessment of how different types of play might be structured, what plays should be about and how they should be performed. The aim of plays was to transport the audience to a parallel reality of 'wonder and bliss'. The stories and the acting were to inspire feelings of love, laughter, energy, anger, fear, grief, disgust and astonishment in the audience. The plays were written in verse. Fifteen types of drama are identified, lasting between one and ten acts. The rules governing the content and structure of an act and its relationship to the play as a whole, are numerous, but essentially all the scenes in an act take place in the same day, and the protagonist of the play appears in the majority. If you are looking for inspiration to expand your ideas about dramatic structure, it is worth reading *The Natyashastra* by Bharata-muni (1951).

Three spliced scenes in Act One of *Osama the Hero* (2005) by Dennis Kelly, performed by Tom Brooke, Christine Bottomley, Michael Mears, Ian Dunn and Rachel Sanders.

Whatever structure or form you choose for your play, remember that it is there to accommodate the magnitude of your ideas. It is there to help you write.

FORM

Structure is the scaffolding that supports your text. It is what bolts together the play's events. Form is the manner in which you write your text. Is it in verse or prose? Does it adhere to a particular genre? Some plays have a familiar structure, but their form is unfamiliar. For example, Dennis Kelly's play *Osama the Hero* (2005) is a three-act play. The first act, which establishes the world we are in and who is involved in the dramatic action, is written in three scenes, in different locations spliced together. One is a monologue set near the bins on an estate, and the other two involve two characters each. A brother and sister are arguing in a kitchen, and a middle-aged man and teenage girl are playing a role-playing game in his garage. Just when we think a pattern has been established as to how we are moving from one scene to another, the playwright breaks it. The second act is set entirely in one location and is entirely realistic, taking place in real time. The third act is a series of monologues that give way to a tapestry of dislocated lines seemingly unconnected but sometimes connected – a distillation of responses to a terrible event. This, in turn, gives way to a very simple, realistic scene between two characters watching the sun rise over Greenwich Park.

Every generation of writers seems frustrated with the pervading structures and forms of theatre they inherit. It is only right and proper that they should feel this way and want to experiment with the possibilities of the medium in order to speak more directly to, and about, their world. It is important, however, as Pablo Picasso said about painters, 'to learn the rules like a pro, so you can break them as an artist'. Aspirant playwrights need to know what has gone before to break new ground. Don't be daunted by the fact that you stand on the shoulders of giants – just remember you do.

INCITING INCIDENT

The inciting incident originates from the Latin word '*incitare*', which means to start up, to put something in rapid motion or stimulate, or encourage something or some character. An inciting incident is a term more commonly used when analysing film than theatre, but it can apply to both. It is usually the event that launches the story. It happens early on in the action. It happens to the protagonist or to the key players in the story, and means something significant to them. It can sometimes precede the start of the play, as in Moira Buffini's play *Silence* (1999), with the banishment of Ymma by her brother from Normandy to Canterbury to marry King Ethelred, or in Hanif Kureishi's *When the Night Begins* (2004), when Cecil invites Jane back for the night. In two of Gogol's plays, the inciting incident is identified in the first line of the play. In his play *Marriage* (1835), a court councillor, Podkolyosin, opens the play sitting on the settee smoking, with the lines: 'Yes, when you're all on your own, sitting around thinking, you realize it's time you were married', and *The Government Inspector* (1836) opens with the mayor informing a number of characters, 'Gentlemen, I have invited you here to let you know some extremely unpleasant news: we are about to receive a visit from an Inspector.' The inciting incident of William Shakespeare's *Romeo and Juliet* happens when the lovers meet and fall in love at first sight at a ball. In *Hamlet* it is the death of King Hamlet. In *Death of a Salesman* (1949) it is Willy Loman, the salesman, coming home unexpectedly.

The inciting incident cannot be ignored and often must be dealt with within a certain time frame. Inciting incidents need not be restricted to the beginning of your play; they can happen in every scene and act.

THE SCENARIO

A scenario gives details of the plot and individual scenes in your play. Not all playwrights see the value in writing scenarios. It can, however, help you to refine the world of your play. It can help you focus the contents and timeline of your story; consider the potential of your locations; identify your main characters, and the internal and external obstacles they face to get what they need; identify the points of conflict and the journeys they take – their character arc. A character arc is the journey a character makes over the course of the story. It can help you decide from whose point of view you are telling the story. Crucially it can help you choose a structure to accommodate the magnitude of your ideas.

GENRE

Genre is a French word that means 'type'. It is a shorthand method of categorization. It is used more often, and more specifically, to brand different types of film and TV shows, than it is to describe plays. There are, however, genres and subgenres that are used in the theatre.

Genres are recognized by their character types, plot elements, structures and themes. They are sometimes used by commissioners, dramaturgs and artistic directors, prescriptively, to suggest ways in which a play should be written. Some playwrights might find this approach to writing too prescriptive and restrictive, for others it is an enormous help. Here are some names of the main genre and sub genres used in the theatre.

There is, of course, tragedy, in which a noble protagonist takes on super-human forces, as Oedipus does in *Oedipus Rex*, only to lose in the process. We empathize with the magnitude of his struggle throughout the play, and we are purged of the negative feelings we have had for the character when they are eventually defeated. Subgenres of tragedy would include 'the tragedy of the common man'. Twentieth-century playwright, Arthur Miller, argued that it should not be a prerequisite

Catherine McCormack and Michael Pennington in *When the Night Begins* (2004) a harrowing thriller by Hanif Kureishi.

Vinette Robinson, Tom Goodman-Hill and Pamela Miles in *Darker Shores* (2009) by Michael Punter, a ghostly horror.

David Hargreaves as Vaughan in *All That Trouble That We Had* (1999) by Paul Lucas – a bizarre black comedy that celebrates our capricious ability to survive in vicious times.

of 'tragedy' that it should concern the fate of a character of noble extraction, it could equally well be the fate of a middle-class character, an ordinary working person like Willy Loman in *The Death of a Salesman*. Willy is deceived by the American Dream, when he realizes he is worth more to his family dead than alive.

Comedy, another genre, has a range of subgenres, which include: high comedy, low comedy, domestic comedy, situation comedy and romantic comedy, to name but a few. Tragicomedy is a genre that combines aspects of tragedy and comedy to make a serious point. Coined in the twentieth century, it accurately captures the tone of many contemporary playwrights and has been applied, retrospectively, to Shakespeare's plays.

Satire is a form of comedy that uses contemporary events in an exaggerated or altered context to make people laugh. It is usually aimed at politics, the hypocrisy of politicians and the pettiness of bureaucratic institutions. Farce is an example of low comedy because it relies more on physical than verbal humour. Parody is closely related to satire but makes fun of another art or cultural form. Melodrama combines elements of both comedy and tragedy. The plots tend to be elaborate with many twists and turns, selected for maximum stage spectacle, with well-defined villains and heroes.

Horror is a genre designed to 'horrify' the audience. There are very few 'horror plays' written or produced. It is hard to know why, since human beings seem to really enjoy a 'safe fright'. Many love the rush of adrenaline, and the release of endorphins and dopamine. We enjoy being able to bear anxiety. The fear of the unknown is one of the most natural and instinctive fears we have. The unknown is also one of our greatest curiosities. It seems there is a very fine line, however, between being able to write something that will frighten people and something that just seems silly. When good horror plays do emerge, however, like Stephen Mallatratt's adaptation of Susan Hill's novel *The Woman in Black* (1983), Andy Nyman's *Ghost Stories* (2010) or Martin McDonagh's *The Pillowman* (2003) they tend to be very popular.

Thrillers, with their various subgenres, like 'psychological thriller', 'action thriller' or 'crime thriller', are defined by the moods they elicit. They, too, can give audiences heightened feelings of suspense, excitement, anticipation and anxiety.

Playwrights tend to give science fiction a wide berth but with the advances in technology, the multimedia resources available to the set designer and the fact that the world seems to be on a mission to self-destruct, there is a need amongst writers to create a plausible future on stage. It was a science fiction play by Karel Capek *R.U.R* (1921) that introduced the term 'robot' to the world. The five plays contained in George Bernard Shaw's (1856–1950) collection *Back to Methuselah* (1922), in which he considers the political changes essential before humankind can govern itself, have been categorized by his biographer Michael Holroyd as science fiction. Many of Caryl Churchill's plays, such as *A Number* (2002) about human cloning and *Far Away* (2000) based on the premise of a world in which everything in nature is at war, might be categorized as science fiction. Alan Ayckbourn has used the genre a number of times in plays like *Communicating Doors* (1994), *Henceforward* (1987) and *The Divide* (2017).

Many subdivisions of all these genres exist.

Tropes

If you are writing in a particular genre, you need to identify its tropes and how to use them. Tropes are plot devices, types of character, images and themes that are incorporated so frequently in a genre that they are seen as conventional (superheroes wearing capes, for example). Be aware, however, that some may have been over-used and if you choose them, your script runs the risk of being accused of being clichéd. The paradox is that you must fulfil the expectations of the genre without this happening. So, read and see as many plays as you can within your chosen genre to familiarize yourself with its tropes, but choose the ones you use carefully. Genres do not stand still, their boundaries widen as writers introduce new elements to their stories.

Deus Ex Machina

This literally means 'god from a machine'. It refers to a moment in some ancient Greek plays when they would literally use a machine to fly in an actor playing a god to resolve whatever problem had been created in the story that the characters couldn't resolve. Aristotle thought it was a cop-out and, nowadays, the phrase is used pejoratively. It refers to any kind of ending that doesn't seem organic to the play – a false event that happens, not as a consequence of the action and conflict. Bertolt Brecht makes fun of the idea of a '*deus ex machina*' at the end of *The Threepenny Opera* (1928) when he flies in the king's messenger on a horse to pardon the criminal Macheath.

PLAYS BASED ON REAL EVENTS

Plays based on real events have a particular appeal for audiences, although biography is not a popular genre in the theatre. Recent examples include *The*

A scene from Robin Soan's verbatim play *Life After Scandal* (2007).

A scene from Tim Luscombe's play *The Schuman Plan* (2006).

Lehman Trilogy (2018) by Stefano Massini adapted by Ben Power, which charts the formation, rise and eventual collapse of the US financial firm the Lehman Brothers. James Grahams' play *Ink* (2017) about Rupert Murdoch's takeover and revitalization of *The Sun* newspaper in the 1960s. J. T. Roger's play *Oslo* (2016), looking at the secret meetings set up by married Norwegian diplomats, Terje Rod Larsen and Mona Juul, to bring together members of the Palestinian Liberation Organization and the Government of Israel to peace talks that no one thought were possible. Lyne Nottage's plays, *Ruined* (2007) about women in the war-ravaged Democratic Republic of Congo and *Sweat* (2015) about unrest in a small American Town, when a group of friends, who once worked together on the factory floor, are forced apart by economic hardship.

Encapsulating the life of a famous person with all their human contradictions is nigh on impossible in this medium. A life is simply too big for the stage. Successful so-called biographical plays concentrate on episodes in a famous person's life to explore a theme that interests the playwright. For example, Peter Shaffer's play *Amadeus* (1979) explores notions of genius versus mediocrity through the relationship between two composers, Antonio Salieri (1750–1825) and his contemporary Mozart (1756–91), *Red Velvet* (2012) by Lolita Chakrabati deals with the biography of nineteenth century actor Ira Alridge, through looking at his approach to the part of Othello. It is sometimes easier for a dramatist to use incidents in a person's life as inspiration for a play about them. For example, Ronald Harwood's *The Dresser* (1979), about the relationship between an actor manager and his dresser, is based on, but not about, his own experience as Donald Wolfit's dresser. Tom Kempinski's *Duet for One* (1981) is about a violinist suffering from multiple sclerosis, like the cellist Jacqueline du Pré (1945–87), but it is not about her.

EXERCISES

Exercise 1 Seven Conflicts

Most plays tend to be based one of these seven conflicts. They will have a protagonist who is battling against:

- *Fate/God*
- *Another person*
- *Themselves*
- *Society*
- *Nature*
- *Supernatural*
- *Technology*

Give an example of two protagonists from plays that you know and describe the nature of their conflict.

Choose a character and the thing they are in conflict with and write three short scenes that identify the source of the conflict, the conflict and the outcome.

Exercise 2 Everything's Fine

Write a scenario where no obstacle impedes the protagonist. For example: A young woman goes up to a drinks' dispenser and buys herself a drink, she has the right change, the dispenser is well stocked and the can is easy to remove. Nearby, friends are passing the time of day on a park bench, enjoying the sun. As she passes them, she offers them some of her drink. They accept it, enjoy it and the birds sing.

Exercise 3 Writing a Scenario

Write the scenario, in bare narrative form, of a play you have written or something you are about to write. Do not write any dialogue. If good lines spring spontaneously to mind, note them down on a separate sheet of paper.

Concentrate on the who, where, what, why and when.

Exercise 4 What If…

Think of a 'what if' situation. For example: What if Sunita were to wake up one morning and not recognize her surroundings. Who is she? Where is she? What if she doesn't recognize anybody she meets, but everybody appears to know her and know what they're doing. Who are they? What are they doing?

And then…

Describe what happens, prefacing each dramatic 'beat' with the two words, 'And then...'. For example: Sunita woke up and wanted to get up, turning on the light and throwing off the covers, she got out of bed, and then she saw that the room was full of people dressed as wood lice and she wanted to get past them but they would not let her pass, so she turned off the light and she managed to pass through them, and then, etc.

Keep us engaged by the story, by imagining that everything that happens is a surprise to your protagonist.

4
PROGRESSING YOUR PLAY

No matter what structure you choose for your play, there are other aspects of playwriting that you will need to consider as you make that sometimes difficult transition from planning to putting the plan into practice.

PLAY TITLES

When you see somebody for the first time, they make an impression on you. So, it is with the title of a play. You make all sorts of assumptions from your first impression. Your title should grab a potential audience member's attention and be an invitation to them to try your play. It should be like the entry sign above a door. It should create anticipation.

A title should have a resonance with the play's story and themes. Many playwrights choose their protagonist's name as the title; for example, Sophocles' *Antigone* (441BC), Shakespeare's *Hamlet* (1600), Henrich Ibsen's *Hedda Gabler* (1891), Molière's *Tartuffe* (1664) and Moira Buffini's *Silence* (1999). Others will name their play after a country or place, like Michael Frayn's *Copenhagen* (1998), David Greig's *Damascus* (2007) or Alistair McDowell's *Pamona* (2014). There are titles that are classical references, like Tom Stoppard's *Arcadia* (1993), Peter Shaffer's *Equus* (1973), Alexi Kaye Campbell's *Apologia* (2009) and David Hare's *Via Delarosa* (1997). Epigrams are popular, like Shakespeare's *All's Well that Ends Well* (1598), Oscar Wilde's

The Importance of Being Earnest (1895) or John Osborne's *Look Back in Anger* (1956). There are yet more titles that reflect the key symbolic motif in the play, like Henrich Ibsen's *The Wild Duck* (1884) and *The Doll's House* (1879), Anton Chekhov's *The Seagull* (1896) and *The Cherry Orchard* (1903) or Simon Stephen's *Herons* (2001). There are titles that can be a line taken from the play, like John Ford's *'Tis Pity She's a Whore* (1629), John Synge's *The Playboy of the Western World* (1907) and Samuel Beckett's *Waiting for Godot* (1953). There are the one-word titles, like Harold Pinter's *Betrayal* (1978), Sarah Kane's *Blasted* (1995) and *Crave* (1998), Anthony Clark's *Wake* (1984), Abi Morgan's *Tender* (2001) and Bryony Lavery's *Frozen* (1998). Then there are the provocative titles that date quickly, but have a certain cachet amongst those writers who want to shock with their work. Titles that swear and blaspheme, like Gavin Davis' *Fat Christ* (2008), Mike Bartlett's *Cock* (2009), Mark Ravenhill's *Shopping and Fucking* (1995), Jim Cartwright's *I Licked a Slag's Deodorant* (1996) and Simon Stephen's *Pornography* (2008). Finally, there are titles that appear to have nothing to do with the play and are simply an invitation to the audience to reflect on the possibilities of what they could mean – something to talk about on the way home, like Eugene Ionesco's absurdist play *The Bald Prima Donna* (1950).

SCENE TITLES

Scene titles can be used in a number of different ways. They can be used to set the time and place for the scene, as in Moira Buffini's *Loveplay* (2001),

OPPOSITE: Jody Watson as Ella in Judy Upton's *Confidence* (1998), where there is serious money to be made amongst the paint-peeling kiosks of the prom.

which follows a trail of seductions, transactions and encounters that take place over 2,000 years, or they can do more than this and tell the story of the scene, as the title does in the first scene of my own adaptation of *Paradise of the Assassins* (2016):

> Scene 1. Winter in the 650th year of Hejirah. Hussain and Zamurrud are doing Hajj – a pilgrimage to the scared house of Allah. In the shadow of the Alburz mountains – in present-day Iran – they come to a fork in the road and disagree about which road to take.

The point of telling the story of the scene before the audience see the scene is to get them to focus not on what is going to happen next, but on how it happens and why. Those of you who are familiar with the plays of Bertolt Brecht will know that many of his scenes are titled this way. The title of the first scene of *Mother Courage and Her Children* (1939) reads:

> Spring 1624. The Swedish Commander-in-Chief Count Oxensteirna is raising troops in Dalecarlia for the Polish campaign. The canteen woman Anna Fierling, known under the name of Mother Courage, loses her son.

STAGE DIRECTIONS

Stage directions convey information about how a play might be staged. Before the eighteenth century, this information was mostly contained within the dialogue of the play. Generally speaking, stage directions are concerned with the scenery and stage effects (sound, lighting, video) but they do extend, on occasions, to describing how actors might move about the playing area and how specific lines should be delivered. In some published versions of plays, they have been added by editors to guide directors and actors in amateur productions. Most stage directions (particularly in plays before mid-twentieth century) are written relative to the position of the actor facing the audience on a proscenium arch stage – right and left are, therefore, reversed from the spectator's point of view – and they are derivative from a period when most stages were raked, or sloped, upwards towards the back. Downstage is towards the audience, upstage is away from them. Directions will relate to characters entering or leaving the space. Traditionally, when an actor is required to leave the playing area, they 'exit'. If more than one actor is leaving the space, you will find some playwrights using the word 'exeunt'. 'Exit', 'exeunt' and 'manet' (meaning to stay) are old-fashioned and are rarely used these days.

In the same way that actors, from an understanding of their character's motivation and who it is that they are speaking to, want to discover for themselves how a line should be delivered, directors don't want to be told by the playwright (unless it is essential to the meaning of the scene) when, where and how they should make an actor sit, stand, or walk. It is only essential if one character directly refers to the fact that they, or somebody else in the scene, is standing, sitting, lying down and so on, in the dialogue. If the physical position of a character is referred to in the dialogue, however, then there is no need for a stage direction. The physical text (e.g. when and where people move, and at what pace) is something that is developed in rehearsal. If it is not clear from the action and dialogue in your script, then it is helpful to know where and when a scene is set.

At the end of the nineteenth century, with an increase in the publication of plays and the number of people reading them, stage directions became more and more elaborate. They were written to set the scene and to describe the intended effect the setting would have on the audience. They set the mood of the scene.

Here is the opening stage direction for Chekhov's *Three Sisters* (1901):

> The Prozorovs' house. A drawing room with columns beyond which a ballroom can be seen. Midday. Outside the sun is shining cheerfully. A table in the ballroom is being laid for lunch. OLGA, wearing the regulation dark blue dress of a high school teacher, carries on correcting her pupils' exercise books,

standing up or walking about the room. MASHA in a black dress, with her hat on her lap reading a book. IRINA in a white dress, stands lost in thought.

Stage directions can be lyrical or sparse, reflecting something of the aesthetic style of the times. These days, in recognition of the creative contribution that will be made by a range of different artistic collaborators – the director, the designer, video artist, sound designer and so on – to the production, playwrights keep their stage directions to a minimum.

Entrances and Exits

In real life, when somebody enters or leaves a room, they do so out of necessity and more often than not other people in the room notice. Therefore, it is important to reflect this in what your characters say and do. Entrances and exits can mark key junctures in a play.

When actors are working on a play, they will often do an exercise to establish their character's previous circumstances, to establish what they might have been doing, feeling and thinking, before they entered the scene. Your characters must have objectives – reasons for coming into the scene, staying in it or leaving. These reasons have to be made clear within the body of the scene. In David Lodge's play *Home Truths* (1998), which is set in a writer's cottage in Sussex, there is a moment in the first scene when one of the characters simply decides to go to the loo, in order that the writer can write a conversation between the two characters that are left. I'm not saying that characters shouldn't be allowed to go to the loo, but there has to be a dramatic imperative for a character to walk out of a scene. The event wasn't foreshadowed in any way.

Time and Place

Whether you are setting your play in real time, in a familiar space or in a fictional location, in an unfamiliar period, it has got to be a credible place and time for the characters to meet. Both time and place should complement and enhance the dramatic action. Ideally, even in the most realistic of plays, the location should also serve as a metaphor. It should have some symbolic significance or relevance, contributing consciously or subconsciously to our appreciation of your themes. Many playwrights, when choosing a location for a scene, think no further than, 'where would these characters be most likely to meet and talk about whatever they talk about, and do whatever it is they do'. Their choices are the obvious ones, shared domestic spaces, like bars, waiting rooms and park benches. Very rarely, however, do the characters in these scenes interact with their environment. The location serves simply as a backdrop and is purely decorative, offering very few opportunities for the actor to explore the subtext that might enhance the impact of the scene. Subtext is when a character seems, from what they say, to have one need but, in fact, has another. It is far more compelling dramatically, if the location can enhance our engagement with what is going on. For example, a scene involving a couple declaring their undying love for each other is likely to be more resonant and compelling if they are lying on a planetarium floor staring at the universe, or trying to make fresh chorizo sausages together, than sitting on a sofa in the sitting room. That said, characters can express subtext by interacting with their environment whilst playing their need. For example, a character might be calmly proposing to another character whilst tapping the arm of the sofa they are sitting on, thereby expressing their inner anxiety.

Wherever you choose to set your scene, at whatever time, it is important to consider on a sliding scale, which of your characters is most comfortable with your choice. A character's familiarity with a space, and attitude towards what time it is, will affect everything that they say and do in the scene. Time, being not just what time of night or day it is, but what month, which season and what year.

As with where you set your scene, when choosing the time, don't choose the most obvious time for the scene to take place, unless it is essential that it takes place then. Learning the facts of life from a parent, whilst combing a busy holiday beach on a sweltering hot afternoon, whilst looking for your younger brother who has wandered off with a large inflatable banana, is going to be infinitely more absorbing than having the same discussion in private in a study.

Bear in mind that a scene played in a public space is very different from one played in a private space. Even if we know the way to, or into, the private space and there is a chance of your characters being interrupted, it is likely to be a much safer space than a public one. Where and when a scene is set will have consequences on what characters say to each other and how they talk.

It is also more captivating for us to listen to characters having conversations when the time for the conversation isn't open-ended. If one character has got all day, then make sure the other one hasn't. An audience is more likely to stick with a scene if you create a time pressure for the characters.

Some plays, usually short plays, are written in real time but most aren't. Plays written in real time are extremely difficult to write. They rarely move locations and are usually no more than one scene or act. As has already been pointed out, it is always a challenge getting characters on and off stage, and most real-time plays have very few characters. They rely upon a number of different devices to get new information into the scene. Perhaps an audio device in the room, email, Instagram, phone or a note left strategically on a table, or there is an open window in the room and other characters can be heard talking outside.

There are many fine examples by playwrights who have managed real-time plays: Arthur Miller's *The Price* (1967), a family drama about the price of furniture and choices made in the past; David Harrower's *Blackbird* (2005), about a young woman meeting her abuser twelve years after the abuse; and Conor McPherson's *The Weir* (1970), set in a rural pub in County Leitrim in the north of Ireland, involving regulars who share stories to frighten an outsider from Dublin, but in the process end up scaring themselves. Like Greek tragedies, there is very little present physical action in *The Weir*, but the storytelling is riveting.

Most plays suggest that chronological and dramatic time differ between scenes but not within them, although this isn't always the case. A whole night is supposed to have passed in Act II Scene 2 of Othello.

It is one of the huge privileges of writing for the stage how much you can play around with time. In a couple of hours, plays can span decades or minutes. In *Betrayal* (1978), Harold Pinter's extraordinary play inspired by a seven-year extra-marital affair, the play uses a reverse chronology. The first scene takes place after the affair has ended and the last one before it begins. In Jane Bodie's play *A Single Act* (2005), about life after a terrorist outrage, the writer deftly dissects two sets of relationships: one running forward in time to its end, and the other backwards to its beginning. It examines how a single political event can change people's trajectories irrevocably.

DIALOGUE

So much of a play's meaning is contained within the dialogue. It is the main means by which the premise is revealed, the characters are identified and conflict expressed.

Dialogue follows from character. Let your characters speak the language of their world. Let their language reveal their thoughts and feelings, assert their individuality and carry their actions. Their dialogue must initiate, change and provoke conflict. It must also express what has happened to the characters and suggest what they are going to do about their situation. When one character on stage speaks to another character, they are invariably trying to affect change in that person.

The writer should train their ear to the peculiarities of the way people speak. The knack to writing great dialogue though, is not just to listen to and repeat real conversations. Most of what people say is punctuated with unnecessary hesitation and repetition, and unless the writer is using this to make a point about the inarticulacy of the character, the result is boring. Dialogue on stage has the feel of everyday speech but it is not mimicry. The art of writing good dialogue is to be selective. It belongs to the contrived, in the best sense of the word, world of the theatre and is actor- and audience-orientated. People in conversations have contrasting voices – so should your characters. Remember, rhythms in a person's speech alternate within conversations.

Throughout the history of the theatre, a stage theatricality, which extends to the type of heightened non-naturalistic language used by some writers, like Caryl Churchill, Martin Crimp and Dennis Kelly, to name but three, can be contrasted with the standard mode of dialogue in British theatre – naturalistic, literal-minded realistic speech. The heightened language these writers use is so personal and stylized that their plays are instantly recognizable as being by them. Words are pressed through the filter of these writers' imaginations. Their dialogue does not always serve a narrative, and often won't be attributed to any named character or characters. The rhythms of their dialogue are judged meticulously. It's as if the writers see text as a musical score and, as a result, along with the words, they have invented a whole set of signs and directions that suggest to the actors how they want the lines delivered. Here are a few that are often to be found under the cast list before the first page of the text:

/ Means the next speech begins at that point.
- Means the next line interrupts.
… At the end of a speech, means it trails off (on its own, it indicates a pressure, expectation or desire to speak)
A speech with no written dialogue indicates a character deliberately remaining silent.

A blank space between speeches in a dialogue indicates a silence equal to the length of the space.
A line with no full stop at the end of the speech indicates that the next line follows on immediately.
Brackets () indicate momentary changes of tone (usually a drop in projection).
A pause is denoted throughout by a comma on a separate line.

Beats, Pauses and Silences

A beat is shorter than a pause, and a pause is shorter than a silence. They occur in plays when a character is lost for words, or taking time to choose their words carefully, or needing to make a decision.

EXPOSITION

Exposition literally means 'the act of presenting to view'. It can also mean 'expounding, setting forth and explaining'. All plays involve exposition at some point – revelations about characters' personalities and their past.

The trick is to make sure that whatever is happening in the present story provokes the investigation of the past and any revelations. Many plays are based on a past story being revealed within a present one. A lot of Ibsen's plays rely on a character's returning and revealing something about the past – *Ghosts* (1882), *The Master Builder* (1893) and *The Lady from the Sea* (1889), to name but three – to resolve the present drama. The word 'exposition' can, however, be used pejoratively when a playwright's dialogue is not justified by the dramatic action.

You are most vulnerable to accusations of unearned exposition at the beginning of your play. The trick is to remember that the beginning of a play, like any other scene in the play, is a point in a larger story, so give the reader or the audience no more than the situation would credibly reveal. By a larger story, what is meant is that when we first meet your characters, they will have a history, and thoughts and feelings for the present, and aspirations for the future, but we don't need to know everything about them immediately. Trust the fact that throughout your play, you will place your characters in situations that reveal things about them, which will give credence to your story and develop its themes.

If a character 'A' in the scene already knows what they are being told by character 'B', and the information is being given solely for the audience's benefit, then cut it unless you can make it clear why B is re-informing A of something they already know.

No beginning is an absolute beginning. All plays start some way into the story, and you need to find ways to drip-feed the audience sufficient information about your characters and their situation for them to be enthralled with what is going on, and eager to find out what happens next. You don't want the audience to get ahead of what is going on and be in a position to predict a character's behaviour. Let them enjoy the process of trying to work things out.

Who Knows What When?

It is difficult, however, when a new character, crucial to your story, arrives in a scene and needs to know what has happened in the play up until that point, to progress the action. Whatever you do, do not put your story on hold while another character fills them in with what the audience already knows. Find a way to make it clear that the character has been brought up to speed with what has been going on before their arrival. Perhaps they could have met someone earlier on, who told them all about it. For example, if we know that character A has had a falling out with character B, but it has been established that they both share a flat with character C, then we are happy to accept that character C will know what has happened, if we are party to a scene in which C is trying to bring about a reconciliation.

SUBTEXT

Subtext has already been mentioned as something an actor can play when there is mismatch between what they would like to be saying and doing, and what they are having to say and do in a scene. Subtext lies under the text, not obvious but nevertheless apparent. Creating subtexts can keep audiences guessing as to when the true motives of a character will be revealed, and so help to maintain their interest in your play. It is a challenge for any writer to decide the extent to which you specify the characters' true intentions in their dialogue. Think about how your character might be behaving in a scene and refine your words to suggest a range of possibilities. Subtext can not only reveal characters' true intentions, it can also reveal their true responses to what they are feeling emotionally and physically in a scene. Often a good actor and good director will identify subtext that you, the writer, hadn't spotted; but they are not to be relied upon to do this.

Dialectics

The Greeks used the word dialectic to mean a conversation or dialogue to discover the truth. The process through which truth was revealed was by a writer or conversationalist making a statement or proposition, which they called the thesis, then contradicting the thesis, with what they called the antithesis. The truth would emerge in the synthesis – the synthesis being a combination of the original proposition and the contradiction to it.

What makes human beings interesting is that we are a maze of contradictions. We experience the world, and progress to maturity, through the juxtaposition of opposites. Characters in plays should progress through the dramatic action, as we progress through life managing to resolve, or having to come to terms with, these contradictory forces.

To be able to create a dialectic in your plays, in your scenes and even within particular speeches, and let the audience figure out where they stand between the thesis and antithesis, is the job of a good playwright. Opposing ideas and feelings should be experienced and examined, and difficult problems confronted.

A dialectical approach to dramatic writing encourages the playwright to compare and contrast characters, ideas, locations and atmospheres. This process intensifies and enriches our experience of the drama. It is dramatically satisfying to have characters with contrasting energies, social backgrounds, identities and viewpoints in a scene.

VERSE DRAMA

Verse drama in Britain is particularly associated with Shakespeare and the playwrights of the English Renaissance. It was an Italian import that resembled classical Roman dramatic texts. The plays were written in blank verse, which is poetry written in a regular metre that does not have to rhyme. Blank verse is most commonly found in the form of the iambic pentameter – five stressed syllables in a ten-syllable line. It is believed to sound close to everyday speech – it does – but it forces writers to be concise and to consider more carefully their choice of words. Encapsulating thought and emotion in blank verse serves the artifice of the theatre well. Stage truth is different from the truth of reality, but it is nevertheless true. It is a heightened, more intense version of the truth. Blank verse remained a popular style of playwriting until the late nineteenth century. From time to time there is a resurgence of interest in writing verse for the theatre, but it never seems to last very long.

SUBPLOTS

Subplots, like verse, are associated more with Renaissance drama than they are with contemporary plays. A subplot is a secondary story to your main story. It usually runs parallel to it and can

be very different in tone, involving a totally different set of characters. It can reflect on the themes of the main story and, eventually, be incorporated into it. Subplots can be used to introduce us to a character's past or to show a different side to their character. They can also be used to support the thesis of your main story.

TENSION AND SUSPENSE

Dramatic action is action that engages and sustains our interest. We are interested in dramatic if we can understand what motivates it. As has already been alluded to, we are further engaged if the motivated action (the need of a particular character or group of characters) is thwarted in some way by an internal or external force or object. Through the dramatic action we witness this conflict and it creates tension, which grabs and holds our attention. Dramatic stories are sustained in many different ways but primarily by building tension and suspense.

Suspense is something we feel when we don't know what is going to happen next. Ideally, it should be something that starts building right from the beginning of your play. From the 'inciting incident' onwards, questions need answering and things needs to be resolved. In order to sustain the suspense, and retain our interest in the final outcome of your story, you should drip-feed us information. The outcome or resolution to your play may be foreshadowed in the plot, but not to the point where it is predictable. Your play may have a number of suspense arcs, as many as there are characters, whose journeys you would have us follow. Conflict between characters can provide moments of long-term, as well as short-term, suspense, as long as the confrontational stakes are high enough. Critics and practitioners talk a lot about 'high stakes' in the theatre. What they mean by this is that, in any given scene, characters must have a lot to win and a lot to lose. It is important in a stand-off between two characters that the stakes are of a similar potency. A classic example of a high stakes' scene is one in

Shakespeare's *Othello*, when the protagonist confronts Desdemona about the handkerchief. Othello has high hopes and antithetically low fears. There are other types of suspense you can create in your play, like giving your characters behavioural traits and then placing them in situations where they don't know how to behave or how to do what is expected of them. A lot of comic suspense is created this way. Dramatic irony is also used to create comedic suspense – when the audience know something that the character on stage doesn't know, and they are just waiting for them to make a fool of themselves. Characters sharing their secrets with the audience, but not with other characters on the stage, can also help build suspense. Right at the start of Patrick Hamilton's play *Rope* (1929), which is based loosely on the Leopold and Loeb student murder case of 1929, we see two characters hiding the corpse of the student they have murdered in a chest. The chest stays on stage until the end of the play, when it is eventually opened by the students' former professor, whose lectures on morality have, as it happens, to a certain extent, inspired the murder. Before this point, the students have held a party for the murdered students' friends and family, and served a buffet dinner off the chest. There is a lot of discussion at the party about what might be inside the chest and all the time we are waiting for someone to open it. The suspense is maintained by us knowing more than some of the characters on stage.

Reversals and Reveals

Reversals and reveals are vital for creating momentum and suspense in a story. If a character's behaviour surprises us, we are curious to get to know them. As soon as we can predict what they are going to do, and why they are going to do it, we are bored. In the interests of holding our attention, given that life can change in an instant, the playwright might want to reverse our expectations of what happens next, either by revealing something new about their character's past or by placing them in an unforeseen situation, or both. Subversion of expectation is essential to drama. Reversals and reveals are common in many plays, particularly thrillers. But you must give the audience just enough to see it coming but not expect it; this is called foreshadowing.

Foreshadowing

Foreshadowing is something that is important to building suspense. It builds anticipation in the minds of the audience about what might happen next. It is when you hint at something of significance in your play, even if the spectator or reader isn't aware of its significance until the final twist or revelation. Foreshadowing can be the key to make sure that your plot reveal is plausible. For example, in Ibsen's *Ghosts* (written in 1881), many of the events at the beginning of the play are only fully understood at the play's end. The long discussion between Pastor Manders and Lady Alving about insuring the orphanage in Act One suggests to us that insurance is going to be important and something is going to happen to the orphanage. Shakespeare's *Macbeth* is rich in foreshadowing examples. All of the witches' prophecies foreshadow later events. The bloody battle in Act One foreshadows the murders later on. When Macbeth thinks he hears a voice while killing Duncan, it foreshadows the insomnia that later plagues him and Lady Macbeth. Macduff's suspicions of Macbeth after Duncan's murder foreshadow his later opposition to Macbeth. In John Steinbeck's *Of Mice and Men* (1937), the killing of Candy's dog foreshadows George's killing of Lennie. The oracle in Sophocles' *Oedipus Rex* (429bc) foreshadows the story of the play.

Good endings should be surprising and inevitable at once.

Flashbacks and Flashforwards

Flashbacks are also used to build suspense. They interrupt the chronological order of the main narrative to take the audience back in time to past events in a character's life. Arthur Miller uses them in *Death of a Salesman* (1949) to illuminate Willy Loman's search for the wrong turns taken in his family's personal and financial history. The danger with flashbacks is that they only really work in the theatre if there is no other way of cohering your present story. Used too often, the story of the past can sometimes seem infinitely more exciting than your present story. Flashforwards, like flashbacks, can be used to cohere your story, by revealing events that will occur in a character's future. In J. B Priestley's play *Time and the Conways* (1937), we are introduced to the dreams and hopes of a group of young people at some sort of party, before we flashforward to see what becomes of them.

Danger

One of the most obvious ways to build suspense is to put your characters in danger. But in order for this to work, you need to make sure that the audience have invested in the character and the degree to which they have invested in them.

A Cliff-Hanger

A 'cliff-hanger' occurs when characters are left in precipitous situations or have a revelation just as the scene ends. We are left asking questions about what is going to happen next. Whenever you have finished a scene, you should jot down on a separate sheet of paper the questions that the scene has provoked.

SCENES WITHOUT WORDS

These are scenes of purely physical action. They are sometimes used at the start of a play as a springboard for the plot, but can appear at any point to summarize, supplement or comment on the action. They were common in Elizabethan and Jacobean drama and known as dumbshows. In Shakespeare's *Hamlet*, Hamlet gets the players to act out a silent, fictionalised version of his father's murder in order to determine Claudius' guilt. They can also be used to physicalize a character's dream, or as flashback sequences to reveal the motivation for a particular action.

RITUALS

Throughout history, ritual and performance have been linked. Rituals involve people or individuals playing specific parts and doing certain activities in a particular order. They are done for and by the community to give meaning to their experience. They involve a prescribed procedure for a religious

A dinner in Act Three of *Our Brother David* (2012) by Anthony Clark, in which David shocks the guests.

or other rite, including stories that have a metaphoric significance and objects with symbolic force. Different cultures embrace versions of different rituals in their drama. These days, the rituals that we share in the west might be considered banal when compared to those of our ancestors. Rituals that commonly appear in plays include getting up, going to bed, meals, working routines, births, birthdays, anniversaries, weddings, funerals, and any number of games and court cases. These rituals provide you with a set of conventions that can either be broken or adhered to for comic or tragic effect. Crucially, they can provide you with a scene structure and a timeline.

SYMBOLS

Words, an object, a location, movement, a time, a colour can all acquire symbolic status when their

Tyrone Huggins as Walter in Lorraine Hansbury's classic domestic drama *A Raisin in the Sun* (1959) presented at the Contact Theatre, Manchester in 1987, the first production in the UK since the year it premiered at the Adelphi Theatre, London.

meaning is beyond what it literally is. Examples might include the tree that is planted in Arthur Miller's *All My Sons* (1947), the plant on the windowsill in Lorraine Hansberry's *A Raisin in the Sun* (1959), the birch twig in leaf in August Strindberg's *Miss Julie* (1889), or Miss Julie's innocent bird that Jean kills without remorse; the forest in Shakespeare's *As You Like It*, or the woods in *A Midsummer Night's Dream.* Symbolism can add depth to your play, drawing an audience's attention to your themes.

THE FIRST TEN PAGES

Given the number of scripts that theatre literary departments, theatre directors and theatre producers receive every year, and the resources at their disposal in terms of time and personnel to process them, it is important to try and hook the reader with your writing as early as you can. Many readers will not read beyond the first ten pages. The first ten pages of your script should set up the world of your play, introduce your main character/s, establish the genre (if you are writing within one) and create conflict. Hook the reader with your inciting incident, with something unexpected happening, something that throws your characters off balance and turns their world upside down. Whatever that is should provoke the reader to ask questions, lots of questions. Like, why did that happen? How did it happen? What are the consequences? A successful playwright will get the reader/audience asking questions after the first page. Look at how many questions are provoked by the opening of Arthur Miller's *Death of a Salesman* (1949) or Moira Buffini's *Dinner* (2002).

Logic

The events in the play must be logical. The playwright must observe the rules of the world they have established. Even if the playwright wants to show the world is inconsistent, they must be consistent in this. For example, at the beginning of *The Bald Soprano* (1950), which Ionesco calls an 'anti-play' the clock strikes seventeen times, and Mrs Smith announces that it is 9 o'clock. Throughout the play, time and human identity are scrambled. There is a character called Bobby Watson who may or may not have died four years ago, and there are lots of characters named 'Bobby Watson'. The end is an exact repetition of the beginning. In *A Dream Play* (1901), August Strindberg's aim was to write a play that imitated the form of a dream – a play not modelled on the pattern of cause and effect, but full of disconnected incidents, totally logical to the dreamer; a play in which memories are either true or invented, and characters split – are present and then nowhere – and time, like the location, is constantly shifting.

Show, Don't Tell

> Don't tell me the moon is shining, show me the glint of light on broken glass.
>
> Anton Chekhov (1860–1904)

It is said that an audience will appreciate your dramatic writing more profoundly if you can get them to use their imaginations to experience what you have seen, heard, thought and felt.

Didactic speechifying by characters who know themselves too well and tell you everything they are thinking, have done and are about to do is boring. Boring because the audience is given no opportunity to interpret the dramatic action for themselves. If there is a disjuncture between what we are told about a particular situation or character and what we then see, we engage actively in searching for the truth of the drama, as we would in a real-life situation. Ambiguity may be the enemy of accountability and progress, but it engages audiences who want to go on a journey of discovery.

As has already been mentioned in Chapter 2, a large part of who we are is expressed in what we do, and characters are better defined in drama through their actions. The word drama has its origins in the Greek word '*drao*' meaning 'to do, make, act and perform'.

When a character is using a monologue, or a soliloquy, to tell us what they are thinking about a particular situation, or something they plan to do or not do, or what they think about a person or group of people, as long as they are travelling with the words, by that I mean using the words to clarify their own thinking, something dramatic is happening. We will go on a journey with the character as they change.

THE USE OF NARRATION AND A NARRATOR

Narration is a technique whereby one or more performers speak directly to the audience to tell a story, give information or comment on the action of the scene or the motivations of characters. Characters may narrate, or a performer who is not involved in the action can carry out the role of 'narrator'.

Tom, in Tennessee Williams' play *The Glass Menagerie* (1944), is a stand-in for the playwright himself and presents the story and is involved in it. The Common Man in Robert Bolt's play *A Man for All Seasons* (1960) plays multiple roles. The Stage Manager in Thornton Wilder's play *Our Town* (1938) is not simply a character in the play; although he doesn't participate in the play's main plot, he is also a member of the crew who is staging the play. He, like so many narrators in plays, exists in more than one dramatic realm. The Narrator in Willy Russell's *Blood Brothers* (1983) does not interact with the characters, but does sometimes speak to them.

In small cast plays that tell epic stories, the role of the narrator is often shared amongst the company. This is a technique used by a lot by writers who have adapted novels for the stage. Both David Edgar's *The Life and Adventures of Nicholas Nickelby Parts 1 & 2* (1980) and Stephen Jeffreys *Hard Times* (1986) use narration shared amongst the company to move the story on between scenes.

Niamh Linehan as Speaker observing Aine played by Jacqui O'Hanlon in *Belonging* (2000) by Kaite O'Reilly. Premiered at The Door, in Birmingham.

The Ensemble in *Paradise of the Assassins* (2016) by Anthony Clark, premiered at Tara Arts Theatre, London.

METATHEATRE

When a play contains elements that draw attention to the fact that it is a play, these elements are called metatheatrical. Elements like a 'play within a play'; for example, 'The Murder of Gonzago' in *Hamlet* or when the fourth wall is broken – the fourth wall being the imaginary wall between the actors and the audience – with the Chorus in *Romeo and Juliet* and in all plays that have narrators. The metatheatrical acknowledges the audience as an active contributor to the theatrical event. Anything in a performance that emphasizes the artificiality of the theatre is considered to be metatheatrical.

ATMOSPHERE

Many production elements will contribute to building the atmosphere of an act, scene or moment in your play. Some of these, such as what time it is, what the weather is like, whether your characters are in an open or confined space, you will have included in your stage directions or made apparent in the dialogue. You might also mention the sounds you hear in the scene and/or the music you would like to underscore the action. Some writers, in tune with the effect particular colours can have on the audience (although whether our sense and understanding of colour is culturally specific or universal is a matter of some debate), will suggest the colour of the walls, the setting or particular articles of clothing.

Good actors, however, responding to well-defined characters placed in plausible situations, can be more responsible than any production effect for creating and sustaining the dramatic atmosphere. Atmosphere is the overall feeling created by a dramatic performance and it is important to remember that your text will need to inspire a group of creative collaborators to give you more of a sense of what you wanted than you could have ever imagined.

THE ENDING

It is, of course, a matter of taste, what constitutes a good ending. A play can end on a sad note, a note of despair and failure, or on a happy and uplifting one. Most comedies have happy endings full of reconciliations and prospects of good fortune; tragedies the opposite.

For Aristotle, the ending of a play needed to resolve the points of conflict in the story and return the audience to 'stasis', reminding them that life continues. It continues, but not in the same way exactly. Something had to have been learnt. The most important lesson being, that people will always triumph over adversity.

There's always a new world dawning at the end of any Greek and all of Shakespeare's tragedies.

The same cannot be said for many twentieth- and twenty-first-century plays that explore the darker sides of humanity, man's inhumanity to man and the relentless moral complexity of our lives, in which moments of happiness and good fortune are only fleeting.

There is a difference between a happy ending and an uplifting ending. The future for the family in Lorraine Hansberry's *A Raisin in the Sun* (1959) is uncertain, but they are a very strong unit by the end of the play. It is hard not to feel uplifted.

The dramatic action may reach a conclusion at the climax of your play but this is not necessarily the ending. The ending is when you tie up all the strands of your plot and have the final word on your thesis. This does not preclude the possibilities of an open-ended ending. Open-ended endings occur in plays where there is no 'climax' to the dramatic action. For example, *Waiting for Godot* (1949) ends with the two tramps convinced, as they were in Act One, that Godot will surely come tomorrow. In Shelagh Delaney's *A Taste of Honey* (1961), at the point at which Jo goes into labour, her mother is about to walk out on her daughter because she has discovered that the father of Jo's child is black, she turns to the audience and asks them what they would do in her situation.

Assuming that you write a climax scene, there are a number of different ways to construct an ending. As a result of the climax, your characters, but particularly your protagonist, can have an epiphany, resulting in a series of revelations that make sense of what has gone before and point to the future. A sudden plot twist can produce the same result. Everything leads up to the ending and once you have written it, everything points back.

It is not always as easy to conclude your thesis as it is to come up with ways of tying up the plot. You need to return to your premise, and focus on what you think you've been writing about. See if you can encapsulate this in one line. Then ask yourself if it is an accurate description what your play is.

A good ending can be an image that encapsulates the whole meaning of the play. In the final lines of stage direction, of Arthur Miller's *The Death of Salesman* (1949), he writes, 'Only the music of the flute is left on the darkening stage, as over the house, the hard towers of the apartment buildings rise into sharp focus.' This symbolic moment shows how the modern world overwhelmed everything that Willy Loman has built. At the end of Bertolt Brecht's *Mother Courage and Her Children* (1939), Mother Courage has lost all three children and her love for them has clearly been in contradiction with her allegiance to war and profit. By hitching herself to her cart in pursuit of another army to cater for, she encapsulates the premise of the play that war and capitalism are intrinsically linked and must be uncoupled for the sake of humanity.

EXERCISES

Exercise 1 Not There

Write a short scene (two sides of A4) for three characters one of whom is not present.
   Or
   Write a short scene (two sides of A4) for three characters, one of whom believes themselves to be in a totally different scene.

Exercise 2 Not Them

Write a scene in which two characters are talking about a third. When the third arrives, they do something that would appear to totally contradict what we have been told.

Exercise 3 Super Objective

Choose a 'super-objective' for a character. A 'super-objective' is what they want to achieve or where they want to get to by the end of your play or in life. Working backwards, list in bullet points ten things that they need to achieve before they can reach their super-objective. Then, between the bullet points, list obstacles to them reaching them and how they ae going to overcome those obstacles.

Exercise 4 The Argument

Character A is trying get an important point across to character B – a life-changing point. Character B is resisting its significance.
   Choose two opposing characters. Write their argument but don't take sides.
   15mins

Exercise 5 Choosing a Location

Choose two characters who are not strangers to each other. One has an urgent need to tell something to the other – it could be that they are in love with them, that a friend has died, that they never want to see them again. Choose a location where these characters are most likely to have that conversation, and write it.
   Then rewrite the scene in a location that demands that the characters have to interact with their environment. A scene in which they have an activity that demands their attention, whilst they are trying to communicate whatever it is they have to communicate. For example, one character is trying to tell the other that they love them, whilst

at the same time wanting to win a game of ten-pin bowling or changing a flat tyre.

Exercise 6 Telling Lies

Write a duologue between two characters that is entirely made up of lies. One at a time, they discover the other is lying.

Exercise 7 Subplot

Chose a story you know well. Write a subplot for it that contrasts in tone but is a different take on the same subject.

Exercise 8 Ritual Exercise

Choose a ritual. Identify the key points in the ritual. Take two characters and, through their behaviour, chart their progress at these key points.

Exercise 9 Subtext Exercise

Character A and character B are at a restaurant ordering food. In the way that they place their order with the waiter, make it clear what the relationship is between them. How does the waiter respond to the way they are treated?

Exercise 10 Claim

Two characters, A and B, find something in a cupboard. They both claim the object is theirs. Using twenty lines of dialogue, write the scene between them. Then write a flashback scene for character A that proves the object belongs to them and not B – again, twenty lines. This scene should involve the same two characters, but you can introduce a third, C. Then write a flashforward scene for character B in which they reveal that they either knew all along that the object wasn't theirs, or they

realized it in the course of the contest with A but didn't want to admit it because of something A had done recently to upset them.

Exercise 11 Action

What is happening here? Using no dialogue describe a scene. The scene should take place in one location. One or two pages. Read the scene and decide which of the actions are important ones for the story you want to tell. Edit your scene. For example: A guy walks into a bar, sits at the counter, orders a drink, the drink arrives, he puts his hand in his pocket, pulls out his wallet and discovers he hasn't any cash.

Edited version: The drink arrives, he puts his hand in his pocket, pulls out his wallet and discovers he hasn't any cash.

What is right or wrong here is determined by the story you want to tell. All actions can be important. The way in which the man walks into the bar could be crucial. What if he is drunk? Rewrite the scene layering the action to reveal which of the actions are important and why.

Rewritten version: A guy sidles into a bar, sits at the counter with difficulty, incoherently orders a drink, finds his pocket and his wallet with difficulty, has three attempts to open his wallet, when he discovers it is empty, he turns it upside down.

Exercise 12 Danger

Think of a character – character A. Put them in a dangerous situation. Write their internal monologue (an internal monologue is a monologue that expresses their thoughts). Then write a speech in which A is talking to another character, B, about the dangerous situation. Let the speech be informed by who character B is and what A wants.

Exercise 13 Dumbshow

Write a scene without words.

5
FIRST DRAFT COMPLETE

If you have been working according to the playwright's clock suggested in Chapter 2, you will have finished your first draft by the end of the eighth month and then not touched it for a month. Now, in the ninth month, you will read your work with fresh eyes and, unless you are very lucky and it says exactly what you want it to say in the way you want to say it, you will start the process of rewriting. For many writers, this is the most enjoyable part of the job – finessing what you have already created.

There are very few playwrights who would dare to say that their work was a work of inspiration that somehow arrived through them and, therefore, can't be messed with. John Osborne (1929–94), one of the first writers to address Britain's status and purpose in the post-imperial age, who was known for his clever, passionate language, was one such writer who never used to revise his work. 'That's it. It happened', he told the management of The Royal Court Theatre, 'It's on the page. I don't know how to change anything in it.'

Even if, for the most part, you are surprised by your own brilliance, resist showing it to anybody else if you know there are things in the text that can be improved upon. However much you think someone else's opinion is really going to help you get to the next stage, however much you want your 'ego' stroked, you must keep it to yourself until you know

that you have got it as good as you can get it. Don't even show it to your closest friend.

Do not be tempted to approach a potential reader with false modesty. 'I know there's a lot wrong with this', when that's not what you really think, 'and it's only a first draft but I wonder if you wouldn't mind… if you have the time… as a close friend… as someone's opinion who I really respect… as someone I can trust… I wonder could you please let me know what you think?'

This is inviting them to find fault with your play where you didn't think there was any. It also puts unfair pressure on them to identify problems that you should be able to identify for yourself.

If you start setting parameters for a reader, for example: 'Would you mind reading this and letting me know whether the plot makes sense?' – it usually means that you know it doesn't. It's almost impossible for a reader to comment on a script without suggesting ways in which they think it can be improved upon. To make the most of any criticism, you need to be confident enough to defend what you have written and know where you want to take your play. If you are not robust enough to take criticism, and too willing to change your script, there is a danger that it will become something you never intended it to be.

There is no shame in working through a number of drafts before showing your play to anybody. Nobody needs to know how many – they won't be impressed by the number. People will only want to read something that you are happy with. Rather than numbering your drafts, keep track of them by putting a new date on your title page every time you start a rewrite.

OPPOSITE: Daniel Weyman and Sian Thomas in *The Glass Room* (2006) by Ryan Craig. In a safe house in the suburbs, human rights lawyer Myles Brody meets with a high-profile controversial historian. She has been charged with denying the Holocaust and he has agreed to defend her.

Somewhere in what you have written is the play you want to write – latent but not yet fully formed. You will find it, if you are prepared to accept that every aspect of your script is up for review.

Start by reminding yourself what you are writing about, why you're writing about it and who you think it might be for. Look at what you have written and check whether the structure serves your content, whether all your characters have a journey and that every line is expressed, succinctly.

Rewriting is hard work. It can involve cutting, redistributing lines and inventing a few new lines. It can sometimes involve having to rejig the play's structure. Your play may or may not need a recognizable structure, but it has to be interesting for a manageable length of time.

The number of actors in each scene, their inferred physical arrangement and the lines allocated to them individually, all contribute to sustaining an audience's interest in what you have written. Think about the shape of your scenes.

Now is the time to start checking rigorously the contrast between your characters, the pace of your scenes, the changing atmosphere in your acts and how easy it is to say the lines you have written.

CHARACTER CHECKLIST

- Interesting human beings exist on many different levels. Are your characters interesting? How are they interesting?
- Do they have a private and a public persona?
- Whenever a character appears in your play, is it clear what they are doing there? What do your characters want? What do they need? How do they intend to get it? What is standing in their way? Is the obstacle internal or external or both? What will they stand to lose or gain if they don't get what they want?
- Have you bothered to name them? Are their names mentioned at least twice in the first few pages to establish them firmly in the

audience's mind? Do different characters call them by different names? Do you have a reason for this? Are you consistent in the use of names?
- What role does gender play in the way your characters respond to the world you have created?
- How far does the past affect the way your characters behave? What is the influence of their parents and their siblings?
- Are they in a committed relationship? People often are but behave as if they aren't, or behave as if they are to avoid another's advances.
- From whose point of view are you telling your story?
- If it is the protagonist's, do they appear in all the scenes? If not, are they referred to in the scenes they are not in? Should they be?
- Are their choices and behaviour influenced by their religion?
- Does race/ethnicity matter to your characters? People of different backgrounds make different choices in similar situations.
- How obvious are your characters' politics?
- The degree to which a character transforms in the course of the dramatic action is often referred to as the character arc. Do all your characters have one? If they don't have one, might they be superfluous to requirements? If they haven't earned their place in the story, cut them. Check this by reading through the play a number of times, reading the lines of one character at a time to check their journey. How much do they change in the course of the dramatic action? What changes them?
- Is it important where they went to school? What work they do? Whatever we learn about a character's past should play a significant part in their present story.
- If they had to share a sofa with another character in the scene, who would they share it with and why?
- Who would they most like to be in the scene with them and who isn't there?

- If someone had to leave the scene, who would they like that to be? Is it obvious in what they say and do?
- Do your characters lie? How economical are they with the truth?
- How far are you standing inside your characters' shoes? Don't tell us what they are feeling but show us. Create situations where we can empathize with what is happening to them.
- Who is your protagonist? Who is your antagonist? How ugly/attractive is your protagonist/ antagonist?

Types, Archetypes and Stereotypes

- Can your characters be identified as types? For example, are they sanguine, choleric, melancholic or phlegmatic? Or a mixture of two or more of these.
- Are they archetypes? Archetypes are types of characters who exhibit certain character traits and are easy to identify by their function in the narrative. Common archetypes include, the Innocent, the Outlaw, the Hero, the Explorer, the Lover, the Clown, the Sage.
- Or are they stereotypes? A stereotype is a simplified and often exaggerated version of a character that is accepted as common by a particular group. Stereotypes can work well in comedy, a genre that often pushes at the boundaries of good taste and appropriateness. When the audience constituency can recognize the character type and can predict how they are going to behave in any given situation, it can give rise to uninhibited laughter. If the stereotype, however, is based on your limited experience and understanding of human behaviour – which most stereotypes would be – you run the risk of being accused of 'political incorrectness', and your audience won't laugh but quickly become bored or take offence. Most stereotypes are negative and to be avoided. As strides are being made toward equal representation in the theatre, racial stereotypes, gender

Paul Bradley as Oliver in the bizarre comedy *All That Trouble We Had* (1999) by Paul Lucas, premiered at The Door, Birmingham Rep.

stereotypes and stereotypical representations of disability are definitely out! Unless, of course, the creative artist is a member of the minority defined by the stereotype and they are using the stereotype as a means of neutralizing the power of stereotypes to obstruct their path to equal participation in society, by reflecting it back to those who conceived the stereotype.

DIALOGUE CHECKLIST

- Does your dialogue advance the action of the play?
- Does the dialogue help your characters achieve their objectives?

- Does your dialogue reflect the state of mind of your characters in a given situation?
- Do different characters have different speech patterns and vocabulary? Is there enough contrast between the characters in your scenes or do they appear to all speak with the same voice? If your writing has a definite style, like Harold Pinter's or debbie tucker green's, and all your characters speak more or less the same way, this needn't be a problem, as long as it is clear that they all want different things, and feel and react in different ways.
- Have you repeated bits of important information you want the audience to understand, three times, in different ways to cement it in their minds?
- Even if the language your characters speak isn't absolutely as they might speak in real life, does it sound real? How far have you tried to recreate realistic-sounding speech patterns, flaws and all?
- Have you over-used your characters' names? Use character names early in your script – at least twice to establish who someone is – and then use them sparingly.
- Check that the beginning of the line doesn't echo the previous line. If it does, does it need to?
- Check whether your characters have earned the right to make speeches.
- Check that the first line of any speech a character makes shouldn't, in fact, be the last one.
- Are you using a character's speech or dialogue to push your own agenda? If you have to tell the audience what the point of the play is, then the play isn't working.
- Don't have characters explain what is happening, create situations in which they can show us.

THE BALANCE BETWEEN PAST AND PRESENT STORIES

- Do we see the thing everybody is talking about, or hear about it retrospectively? Is it more dramatic to have it exist in our imaginations or see it for real?
- Is the present story a continuation of the past story? Have you drip-fed information about the past to the audience only when it is relevant to what is happening in the present?
- How far has the world of your protagonist been upset but what has happened before, or early on, in your play? What does your inciting incident incite? Are the stakes high enough for all of those involved?
- Do the obstacles that your main characters have to deal with in the present story get tougher as the plot progresses? Tougher for some and easier for others, perhaps?
- Does each moment in the present story lead to the next?

STRUCTURE CHECKLIST

- What is the pattern created by the number of people on stage from one scene to the next? Is there enough variation? For example, a two-hander scene, followed by a six-hander one, followed by the three-hander, then back to a six-hander and so on.
- Is there enough variation in the tone of the scenes?
- What is actually going in the scene?
- What will the audience be looking at?
- Does the first line in the scene arrest our attention? Does the last line leave us wanting to know what happens next?

The Ending

Check whether your ending is plausible, and that you do not have to rely on a 'deus ex machina' to provide solutions to the problems you have created. In retrospect, does your ending seem inevitable? Have you tied up all the loose, unresolved strands in your story? Has the ending been foreshadowed? Is it satisfactory? In what ways is it satisfactory?

TIME FOR SOMEONE ELSE TO HAVE A LOOK

Having got your script as good as you can get it, you are now ready to show it to others. You may want to show it to a close friend or send it to a theatre company or to a literary agent or try your luck in a playwriting competition. Whoever you choose to show your work to, choose carefully. If you are choosing to send your unsolicited play to an agent or theatre company, be aware that nine times out of ten your work will be rejected. If you are sending it to a competition, the likelihood of it making the longlist, let alone the shortlist, is extremely unlikely. If you want to succeed, you have to get used to being rejected.

Rejection hurts, but it doesn't have to hold you back. Everyone experiences the sting of rejection, but mentally strong people use that pain to grow stronger. Just because someone doesn't like your play, doesn't mean they're right. Devise your own strategies for dealing with rejection. You may find it useful to remind yourself what started you writing in the first place. You may want to vent your anger to a sympathetic friend or relative. You may want to sit down and rewrite the work or start on something new. The greatest damage caused by rejection is usually self-inflicted. Our natural response to having our work rejected is to become defensive and angry, or intensely self-critical. Whatever you do, be kind to yourself. Even though, for many writers, no amount of praise will ever staunch the blood of some wounds inflicted by unconstructive criticism and rejection, remember the compliments people have paid you and know that in time the intense pain will pass.

Showing It

As well as making sure your play is as good as you can get it before sending it anywhere, and preparing yourself as best you can for rejection, be prepared to wait for a response. Most people who read unsolicited scripts aren't doing it for a living, they have other jobs. Who knows what pressure they will be under, when they receive your script. You have to be patient... very patient. You will be lucky to get an acknowledgement from most people, and it can take months before they actually comment, if at all, on what you've sent them.

To a Friend

In the first instance, if you are showing it to a friend, show it to one who knows how to read a play and knows something about how the theatre industry works. If you think you can trust them to give you informed constructive criticism, you might ask them to consider the following:

- Does the story make sense? If not, where is it confusing? Where does it not add up?
- What does it look like?
- How does it make you feel?
- Who could you see in it?
- Who would you recommend I show it to?

To an Agent

Unless the agency is inviting playwrights specifically to submit unsolicited scripts, there is very little point submitting a new play to an agent.

The point at which to approach an agent is when you are about to have your first play produced and you are unsure about the contract you are being asked to sign with the production company because it appears to deviate, in some ways, from the standard contract templates suggested by the Writers' Guild of Great Britain and Independent Theatre Council (ITC) on their websites. For a small fee, usually a percentage of your royalties from the first production, some agents will cast an eye over the contract for you, to make sure that you are not being taken advantage of. With this arrangement, there need not be any long-term commitment on either side.

Realistically speaking, unless you are incredibly lucky, your royalty earnings from your first play are going to be negligible. No one is likely to want to rip you off, and you'll want to hang on to whatever you can. So, rather than approaching an agent at the contractual stage, send them an invite to come and see the play. Agents are busy people and if they can't come themselves, they are often prepared to send an assistant or will ask to see a copy of the script. Send the script and all the good reviews the production has garnered after it has opened.

Whenever you are contacting an agent for the first time, don't send them a synopsis of your play or the first ten pages. Only send these if they specifically ask for them. Send them a complete draft of the play.

When you approach an agent, know what it is you want from them. There are as many different types of agent as there are types of writer. Do some research online and pick the brains of other writers and theatre professionals you know for guidance. All agents should offer contractual advice and work to get the best deal they possibly can for their clients. There are agreed industry minimum commissioning and royalty rates, but a good agent can negotiate these 'up' and get you additional rehearsal attendance allowances, complimentary tickets and travel expenses.

If what you are looking for is an agent who can give you editorial support and guide your career, as well as always getting you the best deal, they are few and far between. If an agent is offering this support, make sure they have read or seen more than one piece of your work. Hear them talk about your work in detail before agreeing to sign with them. Make sure they understand what you want, and that you understand what they can offer you. Check how far your tastes differ, if they do, in writers, performers, directors, producers and theatre companies. Find out how good their national and international contacts are.

Even if the fit between you seems perfect, you may, in the initial stages of your relationship, want to set targets between you. Remember, they need to make money out of you to support their overheads, just as much as you need them to work for you to earn a living. Review these targets regularly. You don't have to be friends, although many of the best agents are good friends with their clients. Your agent is somebody you should feel you could call upon at any time.

If you haven't received any recommendations from your industry friends, draw up a long list of literary agencies that represent playwrights. A Spotlight publication called *Contacts* and *The Writers' and Artists' Yearbook* will give you the contact details for most. You can also find them in the published editions of most plays and there are some listed in the Appendices. Having identified the agencies, go online and check the writers they represent, or vice versa. Most agencies will have several individual agents who, in turn, will represent a number of clients. If a particular agent appears to share your taste in writers, then shortlist them. Then write to them. Let them know when and where your play is being produced and offer them a complimentary ticket. Keep the letter short – just about what you have done, and why you'd like to be represented by them. Once again, don't send a synopsis of the play. If, in order to entice them to read your play, you want to describe it, keep the description short – a couple of lines, e.g. my play *Nunkhead* (2021) is about two successful businesswomen who take revenge on their school bully with terrible consequences.

Not all agents will accept unsolicited scripts. They will say if they don't on their website. Don't get too disheartened if you don't get a response for ages, if at all. Most successful agents' books tend to be full. You may be better off writing to the agent's assistant. Often, the assistant has more time and energy than their boss and is trying to build up their own list with a view to one day setting up independently.

Trying to get an agent can be a time-consuming business. Take your time. It is not essential at the beginning of your career.

To a Publisher

There is no point in sending your play to a publisher unless it is going to be produced. Having your play published is a thrilling event, because it not only acts as a permanent record of the original production, but contains the possibility of the play having a future life in other productions. Also, a play text can be read, taught and studied.

To a Director, Creative Producer and Producer

Having a director, producer or creative producer attached to your play can sometimes help its chances of being done. Just to know that someone else feels enthusiastic about your work, and is prepared to work hard to see it produced, can do wonders for your ego and confidence. The role of the creative producer is harder to define than that of the director. They are a relatively new phenomenon and there are fewer of them. They can work independently or be attached to organizations big and small, and they are fast becoming a vital part of our national theatre ecology. Their work is more visible than that of the straightforward theatre producer, whose main role is to raise investment from backers and to try and make sure that they see some return on that investment. They will hire a creative team and a theatre, or book a tour. Like the creative producer, they will sometimes generate projects from the concept, but more often than not they will respond to opportunities that present

Play publishing.

themselves, picking up productions and making a commercial success of plays that have already been premiered or revived successfully, and have a proven track record with audiences. Creative producers, whose idea it was to do the play, will want to appoint the creative team and have a large say in the casting and the design.

The best way to get the names of creative producers and producers is to go on to a theatre's website and check who is credited with producing any play in their programme. Then check the producers' websites and make a note of their submission policies.

The relationship between a director and a playwright is the most creative one in the theatre. If you can find a director who is intrigued by the way you look at the world, and enjoys your writing style, it can be a huge step forward to getting your play put on. There are many different types of director, and you will need to work out where they connect with your play and where you connect with them. There may be more, but essentially, there are four different types of theatre director: the deferential director, the deviant director, the daring director and the director's director.

When doing a classic, the deferential director will attempt to present the play in the manner in which it was first produced. When doing a new play, they will defer to the writer's vision for the production. By contrast the deviant director will treat your script mainly as a starting point for a production that is entirely about their vision. Your scenes may be reordered, and dialogue reallocated and the whole event dominated by their conceptual interpretation of your play. Deviant directors are often accused of being gimmicky and over-didactic. The daring director will be the director who will respect what you've written and add to its resonance and impact through their interpretation. The directors' director will use the production of your play to experiment with the medium – to push the boundaries of the art form. They will want to teach and learn more about their craft, the craft of acting, the performer–audience relationship and about the potential of the medium as whole, using your script as a template.

Before approaching a director, check what their work is like. To be fair, given the precariousness of the profession, directors tend to be quite eclectic in their tastes and approach to styles of production. Their approach, more often than not, being defined by the resources available to them and the tastes of the artistic director or producer who is employing them. It is hard to pigeon-hole most directors.

Some, however, will have a signature style, which is identifiable from all their productions, which you might have seen, read or heard about. If you like their style, there is no harm, whatever their status, in sending them your script via their agent, preferably by email, 'for the attention of… whoever the director is'. Their agent's information should be readily available online. The agent may or may not forward it to their client, depending on how busy that director is. If the director trusts their agent's taste, they may expect them to read it first. There is no guarantee that you will get a response with this approach, but if you flatter the director by identifying what it is about their work that you like in your covering letter, there is a chance you will. At the very least your approach should be acknowledged by the agent. Directors are two a penny. Make a note of who has directed every production you see. Learn something of the director's craft, so that at any meeting with a director you can hold your own.

Most directors at the start of their careers, like playwrights, don't have agents until they have had something put on. If there are directors you know and trust from university, or from youth theatre, or from hanging around chatting to people in theatre foyers and cafés, ask them if they might be prepared to read and talk to you about your play. Amongst young theatre directors, the fashion swings between wanting to give priority to directing new plays and doing innovative productions of the classics that speak to our times. Approach a director who shows some interest in new writing.

Be aware that if your play is eventually picked for production by a theatre management, a creative producer or producer, you have a right to be consulted about who directs it, but you will not have the final say. Don't promise the play to anyone.

To a Theatre

Be wary of sending your unsolicited script to a theatre that rarely produces a new play in its main programme. Do your research and identify those theatres and companies that regularly produce new plays (see Appendices). Check whether, alongside their main space programme, the company runs a youth theatre or a community participation programme. Both of these activities usually support new writers. The important thing is to get your play on wherever you can, and to learn from the experience.

There are few theatres interested in new writing who are prepared to accept unsolicited scripts all year round. Look on their website for times when they invite submissions. They will probably acknowledge receipt of your script, but won't guarantee you any sort of feedback, unless they are interested in meeting you. Be prepared for the email that says 'if you haven't heard from us within three months we're not interested', or words to that effect. The reasons why most theatres can't provide the reading and feedback service they once did for aspiring playwrights are largely economic. The theatres are no longer staffed at the same level that they once were, and there are many, many more people writing plays, and fewer productions being mounted annually.

There are many freelance directors and dramaturgs offering an online reading service and dramaturgical advice for a fee. Check their references before approaching them or parting with any money.

Some theatres still insist that you submit a hard copy of your play. Most, however, will accept an electronically submitted script. There is no excuse if you are submitting your play electronically for it not to be acknowledged.

Competitions

There are a number of playwriting competitions run each year by organizations trawling for new plays. Most competitions are intended for emerging playwrights and so it is not possible to win a competition twice. Read the competition guidelines to understand what sort of contract you are committing to should you be a winner. If you have to pay to enter the competition, check the history of the organizer and make sure what you are getting for your money. At the very least, they should offer you some written feedback as evidence that your play has been read. Check what exclusive rights they want on your work should you be lucky enough to win; usually, this is in the region of eighteen months. Your prize money should be paying for this option and should be the equivalent of a minimum commission charge for the scale of the producing organization.

In order to meet a competition deadline, do not enter the competition with a draft you are not pleased with – you will only be disappointed. Whatever the rules of the competition, it is worth bearing in mind that the organizers have to think about the practicalities of putting on the winning play. In most places, the main constraint is cast size. Across most theatres, both professional and amateur, the viability of producing a play drops very quickly as the cast size increases. If there's one bit of fine print you need to check, it's this one. You don't want to write a twelve-hander for a competition and then discover the limit was six. As well as cast size, if the competition is being organized by a theatre company, and most are, your play's suitability for the performance space will inevitably be an issue. Just as you would familiarize yourself with a theatre's programme before submitting an unsolicited script to them, research what the personal preferences are of those in charge of the organization running the competition, and the judges. Different theatres have different tastes in what they programme, and that will influence their choice of winner. Remember that competitions are a lottery, and if you win, it's a bonus. Don't pin

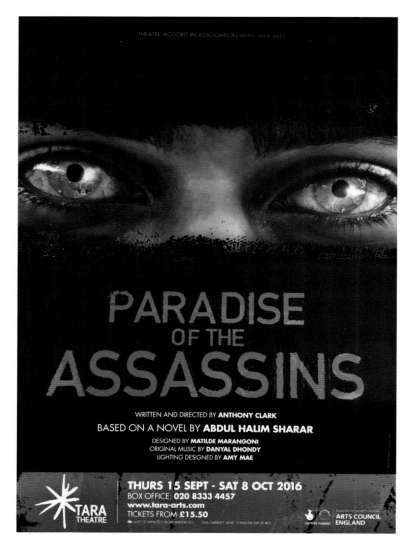

Paradise of the Assassins poster.

all your hopes on the phone call that may never come. Whilst waiting for the results, keep writing and, if you don't win, don't give up. You will have done very well to get any free feedback.

THE WAIT

Once you have submitted your play and it has been acknowledged by the recipient, you must be prepared to wait. A busy agency, producer, competition organizer or theatre company will then distribute it to a reader. The reader will have been briefed to read a certain amount of the script before making a decision about it. As already mentioned, it is not uncommon for a script to be rejected if the reader can't identify anything distinctive about the writing in the first ten pages.

Assuming that your script has been read-through to the end, carefully, the reader will then report on it. Traditionally a reader's report will be a written one. A familiar form of script report will outline the play's plot, identify its themes, quantify the practical requirements needed to mount a production and assess its relevance to work that the organization is already doing, and contain some comments for the writer. The reader will also recommend to their employer how to proceed with the script. They may suggest it be rejected outright or rejected with an encouraging letter offering you some feedback. They may see promise in the writing and want to meet you to discuss what else you're working on. Or, they may call you in for a meeting to say that they are seriously interested in doing your play, but they'd like to see some rewrites.

THE FIRST MEETING

If you are called in, you are unlikely to be meeting the first reader of your script, but a literary manager, dramaturg or director.

Literary Manager

A literary manager is someone who manages a group of script readers, and reads and evaluates plays for a theatre company that has a particular interest in new writing. Not all theatres have literary managers. Unless that script is something the theatre has commissioned, they will not be the first person to have read your script. They manage the commissioning process, as well as any redrafting of non-commissioned plays. They sometimes have early meetings with writers and follow their career paths until they are in a position to work with them. Occasionally, they will feed ideas to writers with a view to commissioning a play from them. They network with agents.

Dramaturg

A dramaturg will be responsible for many of the same jobs as a literary manager, but they will also often sit in on rehearsals providing contextual research for the production. They will support the writer's position in the rehearsal room. They will help with any editing that needs to be done, and provide notes for the programme. A good dramaturg will be encouraged to participate in season selection with the theatre's senior management team, and they will curate complementary activities (talks, events, Q&A sessions) around the production. Dramaturgs are not particularly common in the UK; their job usually falls to the director, the assistant director or the theatre's writer in residence.

Potential Director

The director who is interested in new writing will often approach your script in a much more practical way than a good literary manager or dramaturg. They will ask questions about the world of your play and how you see certain bits working. They should be educating you about your play, just as much as you are educating them. They should be interested in the words and be able to identify the patterns you have made with them. What they will be offering is an interpretation of your play. Check how clear this interpretation is by quizzing them about what they have understood of the play. Some, but not all directors – often those that are the most enthusiastic about what you have written and would like to direct it themselves – will start offering you ways in which they think you could improve your script. These 'script doctors' are to be listened to, but be careful about the degree to which they want to change your play.

Assuming your first meeting has gone well, one of a number of things could then happen. They could send you away feeling very positive about your play and want to see what you write next; they could decide not to do the play you submitted but want to commission to write something else; or, they could decide to commit to doing your play and give you a production date.

Contradictory Notes

Be aware that you may get contradictory notes from people who read your play. Don't accept the notes from the person who is most likely to do your play unless you agree with them. If the literary manager and director from the same organization are offering you different advice as to how to progress your work, let them know.

THE COMMISSIONING PROCESS

If the company or producer is interested in commissioning your next play, there will follow a meeting or a series of meetings between you and them, in which together you explore an idea and agree on the parameters of the commission (e.g. cast size, scale of production, target audience, timeline and so on).

Within both the commercial and state-subsidized theatre in the UK, the commission fee is dependent on the play's length and the commissioning organization. Fees are paid in three instalments: on signature, on delivery of a fast draft, and at the point at which the organization commits to doing the play. The last of these three payments is in lieu of royalties. The remaining royalties, which are calculated as a percentage of the box office on an average length of run of four weeks, should be paid to you or to your agent within twenty-eight days of the last performance. If the play is on for much longer, then a separate royalty payment schedule should be negotiated. Rates for commissioning royalties change from year to year and can be checked on the Writers' Guild of Great Britain's website or that of the Independent Theatre Council. The commissioning organization is obliged to get you a production date within ninety days of agreeing to do the play. After this point, their option lapses and the performance rights revert to you.

They Commit

If the producer commits, immediately, to doing your play, then they will have to pay you to option the rights for a set period of time, rather than pay you a commission fee. The option fee is negotiable, and the agreement you sign with the producer acts as a licence to do the play within an agreed time frame. If the organization that wants to programme your play is a subsidized company, then this option fee should not be less than the first two payments of a commissioning contract. It is likely that they will want rewrites from you and, therefore, you are, in effect, entering a commissioning contract with them, with the first two payments being paid up front. In the commercial sector, the option fee is likely to be less, but there is a chance that the play will run for longer and your royalties will amount to much more than they would in the subsidized sector. Whatever contract you sign with the producing organization, subsidized or commercial, always check the dates of their option. Never, never sign an agreement that gives away the rights to your work in perpetuity.

COPYRIGHT

Copyright is a law that gives you ownership over the things you create. You own it and it's the copyright law itself that assures that ownership. The ownership that copyright law grants comes with several rights that you, as the owner, have exclusively. Those rights include the right to:

- Reproduce the work.
- Prepare derivative works.
- Distribute copies.
- Perform the work.
- Display the work publicly.

These are your rights and your rights alone. Unless you willingly give them up, no one can violate them legally. This means that, unless you say otherwise, no one can perform a piece written by you or make copies of it, even with attribution, unless you give them permission. You or your agent license your play for performance.

You don't have to apply for or pay a fee for copyright. There isn't a register of copyrighted work in the UK. You can mark your work with the copyright symbol ©, your name and the year of creation. To prove that your script was created in the year you say, put it in a sealed envelope and send it to yourself. Do not open it.

Copyright for dramatic work in the UK lasts for seventy years after the playwright's death. Your work copyright should be protected in other countries through international agreements.

Make sure that there is a clause in any contract you sign with a producing organization that makes it clear that you have the moral right to claim authorship of your play. There should also be a clause in the contract that stipulates that, in the event of additions to the script being made in development or rehearsal by dramaturgs, directors

or actors, such additions must be subject to your approval and will accrue to your moral rights.

Do not assign your copyright, unless you can't see a way of spending the money you're being offered in a lifetime!

REHEARSED READINGS

If you are offered a rehearsed reading of your script, check what it is the producing organization hopes to discover from the process and know what it is that you are hoping to find out. You can be offered a rehearsed reading of an unsolicited script, but you are more likely to be offered one in the latter stages of the commissioning process. Sometimes the producing organization don't feel that they can commit without hearing it in front of a small audience. Sometimes they organize the reading to enable you to hear your play and to make the play better. Sometimes though, they have already decided not to do the play but want you to feel that they have given it every opportunity

Vicki Pepperdine and Helen Baxendale not getting on in a scene from *Amongst Friends* (2009) by April De Angelis.

to prove itself worthy of production by putting it in front of people. In effect, the reading is fobbing you off. People responsible for making artistic programming decisions should be able to judge a play without having to hear it read aloud.

The rehearsal time allotted for a rehearsed reading is often no more than half a day but can be anything up to a week, depending on the resources of the company. If you are offered a rehearsed reading, make sure you are offered a good-quality cast. A number of well-known good actors are more than happy, if they are not working, to offer their support to a new project by coming to read it. In the same way that good actors can paper over the cracks in a play, bad ones can totally miss what's there. A rehearsed reading is not an opportunity for a director to show off their staging skills. The simpler the better. Place two rows of chairs, one behind the other, with gaps between the chairs. The gap between the chairs in the back row should be far smaller than the gap between the chairs in the front row. The actors sit on the back row when they are not in a scene and come to the front to join one. The reading of stage directions, by either the person who has organized the reading or the actors to whom the directions refer, should be kept to a bare minimum. The event is about showcasing the play, not the acting talent. The audience, and it's usually made up of theatre practitioners or investors, need to be able to understand the story, get a measure of the tone of your writing and to identify a target audience. If there is a question and answer session after the reading, make sure that it is properly chaired by somebody who has your best interests at heart.

WORKSHOPS

If you are offered a workshop on your play, be sure to understand what it is whoever is leading the workshop wants to explore. The best workshops for a playwright are those that not only reveal any faults in your writing, but explore ways in which it can be improved. A workshop can be a pleasant enough social experience for the writer but not a particularly creative one, if the whole time is spent exploring how to stage particular moments. Some of the benefits of having your play workshopped include the fact that you will receive creative input from others, and their energy and commitment rubs off on you and gives you the confidence to move forward with the next draft. If the workshop is led by an insightful practitioner, you will have been able to identify what does and doesn't work about your script and come away with a plan to make it better. A word of warning though, the best contributors (actors) to a workshop are not necessarily those who would be ideally suited to playing the parts you have written. For a workshop, you want skilled, versatile actors with inquisitive minds and strong opinions.

The Workshop from a painting.

DEALING WITH FEEDBACK

In whatever way you receive your feedback, it will more often than not start with identifying things about your play that work, before criticizing things that don't, and then going on to suggest ways that things can be improved. Good feedback will ask you a series of questions, to help you to identify where and how you can improve your script. Be sceptical of the feedback that didactically states, categorically, what needs to be done to improve matters. Learning how to make the most of feedback takes time, especially if it is critical.

Face to face meetings can be particularly daunting – for both parties. Your initial reaction to any criticism is likely to be defensive. So don't react straight away, just nod, say, 'thank you, I'll think about it' and move on. Later, you might find a nugget of truth in what has been said, or simply reject the criticism and hope they'll have forgotten what they said to you by the next time you meet. Don't interrupt the person giving you their feedback. Remember the positive advantages of feedback and how much you wanted it. If there is anything in the feedback that you don't understand, ask for clarification, but, ask in a way that isn't confrontational. Put yourself in their shoes, if you can. Then check whether they'd be happy to read your script again once you've managed to incorporate their feedback. If so, when? If they don't want to read it again, but would be happy to see your next play, say 'thank you' and take the positive from the meeting. Nobody would be offering you feedback of any sort unless they were, at some level, interested in your writing and encouraging you as a playwright.

EXERCISES

Exercise 1 A Personality Test

Give your characters a personality test. Choose an online personality test and answer for your characters, to decide what type of person they are, and under what circumstances they function well or feel threatened.

Exercise 2 Visualizing Structure

Orientating a sheet of A4 that has been divided into squares (30×30 squares approx.), to landscape, draw a line across the centre of the page. Above the line, starting from the line and going up vertically, number the squares 1 to 15. Do the same below the line, again starting from 1. So, you have two pillars of numbers 1 to 15: one above and one below your centre line. Across the top of the page, fill in the number of scenes in your play or page numbers when characters go on and off. Then, for each scene, mark the number of characters in that scene by filling in the squares above and below the line. You will end up with something that looks like a sound graph. This will help you to identify how much variation there is in the number of characters that are on stage throughout the play.

Exercise 3 Show Report

Write a show report for your own script or that of a friend.

6
PRE-REHEARSAL

Before the rehearsal period begins, the director and the playwright will meet many times, usually at the instigation of the director, to go through the text and share each other's vision for the production. Be sure to identify the things in your script that really matter to you.

The playwright should make themselves available and be given the opportunity to meet some of the other creative collaborators involved on the production, particularly the designer. I have never directed a new play where the designer hasn't insisted on meeting the playwright.

The marketing department, or the person responsible for selling your play, will want you to have an input into their plans. It is in your interests to be as helpful as you can to those who are responsible for selling your play, but remember that your first priority is to deal with anything that emerges in rehearsals. Decide whether you will or won't give interviews and, if you do, how many and to whom? You should definitely be consulted about any image and copy they are using in any publicity material – this should be stated in your contract.

Collaboration always involves an amount of compromise, but you should look on this as something positive. Be prepared to rethink your expectations and show your appreciation when someone has had a better idea than yours. There are two kinds of loyalty expected from any collaborators in a creative process: a public and a private one. Be sure you can offer both.

OPPOSITE: Kate Fleetwood as Tash, after a night to forget, in Abi Morgan's *Tender* (2001).

WORKING WITH A DIRECTOR

In most production processes, the director has the final say on all the design elements, the cast and how the script is to be interpreted. Sometimes the final say will be with the creative producer or producer, especially if they have to answer to their investors. It is in their interests to work closely with the director and vice versa.

The playwright is contractually entitled to have a say in who directs their play, but you don't have the final say. The four types of director, that have already been identified in Chapter 4, fall into two camps. In the first are those who serve the playwright's vision, and in the second those who use all of the elements of the theatre, of which the script is merely one, to fashion their own work of art to serve their vision. Know who you are working with. Make sure you spend enough time with the director, to gauge whether they understand your intentions and whether you understand theirs. Make sure that you are in a position to judge their 'people' skills.

As an emerging playwright, if you are offered the opportunity to interview a number of directors, don't agree to do this on your own unless you are sure you know what a director does, you have seen the applicant's work and you are confident in your own abilities to assess personality, quickly. Prepare a list of questions for the director and be willing to answer their questions, honestly.

Make it clear that you don't want to do the director's job for them, but that your main concern has always been narrative clarity, that the emotional through line of your characters should be understood and interesting, and that you want your ideas to encourage the audience to see the world in a new light or to think harder about what they already know. If you just want people to have a good time, let the director know in what way you want them to enjoy themselves.

Pre-rehearsal, the closest creative relationship the director will have with any member of the production team, besides the playwright, will be with the designer. In rehearsal, it will be with the actors.

THE DESIGN TEAM

It is extremely unlikely that you will be consulted about the choice of the whole design team for your play. They can be brought together by the creative producer but, more often than not, they are chosen by the director. The director will want to work with people who they already know will go the extra mile for them, or someone new whose work has impressed them, or someone who, by association, will give the production the quality stamp. A lot of the design team's work is

done prior to rehearsals, but expect it to continue through the rehearsal period up until the press night.

The Set Designer

A set designer is responsible for designing the set, working closely with the director and the design team to create the world of the show. The director may or may not invite you to the early meetings they have with the designer, but you will be invited at some stage to discuss the design. When you are invited, you may be shown any number of ideas, sketched or in three dimensions, in rough models or on a computer. It is extremely unlikely that you will be shown anything that is 'just as you imagined it'. Depending on how much you trust your own visual imagination, take your time to respond. If you are not sure what you are looking at, always ask. General questions at first and then specific questions as to how they see certain moments in your play being staged. The director and designer may be able to answer these questions off the top

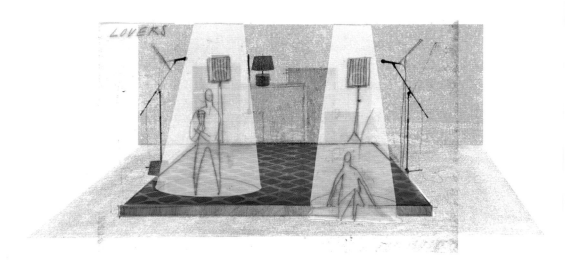

"Lovers" white card set proposal

Jessica Curtis's design drawings for *She*, by Anthony Clark; seven short, two-hander plays in one, in which two young women reflect on women at different ages.

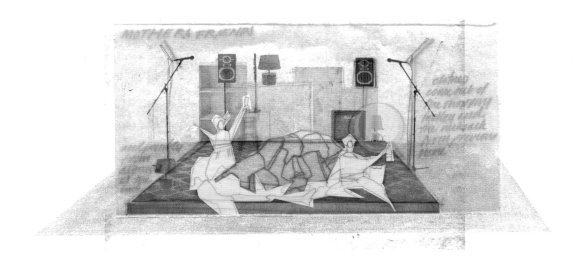

"Mother's Friends" - white card proposal

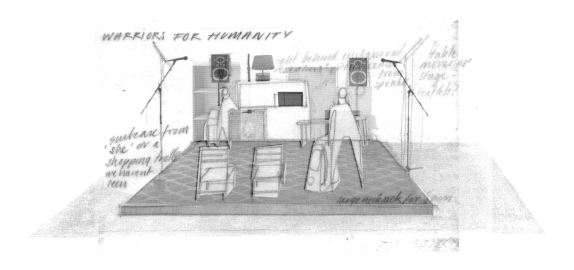

"Warriors for Humanity" white card set proposal

Jessica Curtis's design drawings for *She*, by Anthony Clark; seven short, two-hander plays in one, in which two young women reflect on women at different ages.

of their heads, or they may refer to a storyboard that they have worked on or move figures around in a model box. A storyboard is a graphic representation of how your play will unfold, scene by scene, or from one event to the next. Rather like a comic novel, it is made up of a number of squares with illustrations or pictures representing each scene, with notes about what's going on in the scene, what the atmosphere should be and how sound and lighting will contribute to this.

You may not be given any say in the design you are being offered. In which case, you will have to trust that the director and the designer know what they are doing, and if it doesn't delight immediately, hope that it will grow on you when you see how it is being used in rehearsal and performance.

Good theatre design is design that responds to the text by creating an environment that the actors can interact with in order to reveal your narrative, and the meaning and emotional impact of your play. Conceptual design, which tells the audience what the play is about before they have had a chance to discover it, is something to be avoided. A good design will reveal itself through the performance. It will invite the audience to explore the world of your play.

Once the design has been agreed, and the designer has completed their technical drawings for the workshop, building work on the set can start. Work on realizing a stage design usually starts well before the rehearsal period. It is very rare, given the programming demands on most theatres and the average length of rehearsal periods in the UK (four to six weeks), that the actors will get a chance to play on the real set before the technical week. The technical week is when all the technical aspects of production are brought together.

You may work with someone calling themselves a scenographer, rather than a set designer. A scenographer specializes in designing all the visual elements of a performance, including lighting, sound, animation and costume. Most designers in the UK don't train as scenographers but are expected to design both set and costume. Given the workload on a really big show, the roles are often split.

The Costume Designer

A costume designer is responsible for designing the costume, hair and make-up for a production, working closely with the set designer to ensure that the costumes fit the world of the production. They will often create designs ahead of the production being cast, and have to make significant changes to their designs when they meet the performers. Depending on the status of the actor, and their physique, they can be very fussy about what they are going to wear. Matching shape to size and colour to skin tone is important if you want the actor to feel confident in what they are doing.

The Lighting Designer

A lighting designer is responsible for designing the lighting for a production, working closely with the director and the design team to create lighting states for atmosphere and mood on stage. The lighting designer will often have an initial idea about how the lighting will look for a show and will then make adjustments during the rehearsal process. Once their design work is complete, technicians will rig and program the lights. Stage lighting is computer-operated and it takes a phenomenal amount of time to program what each light is going to be doing in every scene. A skilled assistant lighting designer who can program a computerized lighting board, quickly, is a great asset in the technical rehearsal.

The Sound Designer

A sound designer is responsible for designing the use of sound within a production, e.g. sound effects and/or music. It is very rare for a show to have live musicians playing in it unless it is an 'actor musician' show or the producing company can afford to pay musician union rates. They will work with the director to create and develop sound that locates and enhances the action in your play, and generates atmosphere. They will also advise the director on whether the production requires microphones and where the sound source should be placed (i.e. speakers).

It is rare that a company will be able to commission music especially for your play. Some sound designers will happily take suggestions from the director and playwright; others will want you both to respond to their ideas.

Many sound designers are keen to build a continuous soundscape for your play. A soundscape is a combination of sounds that can be used to locate scenes, literally (e.g. birdsong and running water to suggest we are outside near a stream), or a blending of abstract sounds to enhance the emotional impact of the scene. These sounds work on an audience subliminally, and they only become aware of them when they are not there. Turning a soundscape off is the most effective way of getting the audience to hear silence.

It is the producer's responsibility to obtain the rights for any music that is included in your script and in the production of your play. Most entertainment venues have a subscription to the Performing Rights Society, and a record is kept by them of any music used in the productions (what is used and for how long). The producing company is then charged a royalty. In some cases, permission to use music needs to be granted in advance. The artiste may want a credit. Some bands are weary of their music being used to promote products and causes that they don't approve of.

CASTING

A playwright is entitled, contractually, to be consulted about casting, but again does not have the final say. If you have not specified a particular age, race, gender, colouring or size in your cast list, the stage directions or in the dialogue of your script, encourage the director to be open-minded when considering the actors for a part. If you have specified certain physical features about your characters, ask yourself how important they are to your narrative and thesis.

In the commercial theatre, final decisions about casting are made by the producer or creative producer having consulted with the director, the casting director, and the playwright. Depending on the professional status of the writer, they could have more of a say on the casting than the director. If, for example, there was a debate between Tom Stoppard and the director about which actor would be better for a particular part, the playwright would have the final say.

In the subsidized theatre sector, the freelance theatre director will make the decisions in conjunction with the casting director (although not all theatre companies can afford casting directors), supported by the artistic director or project producer.

A casting director is someone who organizes and facilitates the casting of actors for the roles in the play. They can be used to help cast the whole company or any part of it (i.e. the two leads). A good casting director should have a thorough understanding of the play and what the creative team are after, as well as knowledge of industry trends and available acting talent. They should have the interpersonal skills to communicate to actors' agents and to the actors themselves, and be able to suggest a range of suitable actors for any part. As well as arranging and conducting interviews and auditions, they are sometimes required to negotiate fees with the agents on behalf of the management that is employing them.

The playwright may be asked by the casting director to write them a synopsis of the play, and a short character breakdown of all the characters. They will use this information to send out to agents and other casting services.

In audition, the actor may have prepared a speech from your play to present to you, the casting director and director. Or they may have been asked to prepare a speech from an extant play that is similar in style and tone to yours. They may be asked to read a scene from your play with another actor or the casting director, or even with you. You are not obliged to stand in if the management haven't got anybody to read with the actor. Depending on how many rounds of auditions the management are doing, the director should find time in the process to quiz the actor on how much they have understood about your play, and what are their thoughts on your thesis. This is sometimes very revealing for the playwright. It can be an early indication of things that are still unclear in the script.

There is no set number of times an actor can be seen for a part, before they are either offered or rejected. However, given that they are not paid to audition, and are rarely reimbursed their expenses, it seems unfair to call them back more than three times. If a director is planning to see an actor a number of times, don't expect to be with them at every meeting.

Remember that during the audition process, the director is not only assessing the actors' ability to meet the specific demands of your play – their appearance, their physical and vocal technique, their ability to embody a character, and their understanding of, and commitment to, your play – but also how they are likely to operate in a rehearsal situation. After all, they are going to spend however many weeks of their life in a room with that actor and other actors, and it is important that the rehearsal process is energized, creative and fun. The director will be checking their 'directability' in the context of an ensemble of actors in a collaborative enterprise.

Star Casting

Casting well-known names from TV or film in your play can be a useful way of drawing attention to it, and a way of generating ticket sales, but it has to be the right star in the right part. Always check what the star is known for and whether they have significant theatre credentials. They have to be right for the part. Working in the theatre is a gruelling business and they have to have the stamina.

Colour-Blind and Colour-Conscious Casting

Casting is a political issue. The debates over so-called 'colour-blind' and 'colour-conscious' casting have been heated over many, many years,

especially when a theatre's decisions do not align with a playwright's wishes. Sometimes directors may decide they can give their interpretation of your script extra resonance through racial casting. This is called conceptual casting. Others may decide to ignore the race of the actor as long as they all sound white! This is called colour-blind casting. It is unlikely to happen on the first production of your play but some directors may ask you to transpose the cultural setting of your play, depending on the context in which it is being performed, to make it more accessible to its audience. This is called trans-cultural casting. Lots of directors in the interests of diversity will do what is called societal casting. This is when an actor of a minority race is cast in a part that mirrors where they might be seen in society, e.g. an East Asian actor playing the part of a care-home nurse. Perhaps the most exciting approach to casting is an intra-cultural one, where actors are asked to express their own culture in the parts they play, without any attempt to create a unified world through the way an actor looks and sounds. Directors who are interested in this way of casting plays understand that there are many aspects of the theatrical experience that do not rely on naturalistic representation. For example, the relationship between a brother and sister on stage can be understood, and resonate, on stage without both actors sounding and looking the same.

It has been the policy of Equity, the actors' trade union, since 1963 that no actor should be discriminated against on grounds of race, gender, sexuality or disability. It is a matter of some debate whether race-neutral new plays have led to many more opportunities for actors and writers of colour, and contributed to a more diverse demographic in the audience. Paradoxically, there are playwrights who now insist on defining character identities more specifically in order to steer managements away from their default position of casting white, cisgender, ability-typical actors for every role. They also insist on a more authentic casting, to yield more authentic representation of character, i.e. if the character is mixed ethnicity

Poster for Sarah Wood's play, *Nervous Women* (1992), a play that parallels the life of a modern woman coping with unemployment, with that of a Victorian wife with growing agoraphobia.

Japanese-African-American-Ethiopian non-binary, so should the actor be. The problem then arises when communities are never exposed to the viewpoints of certain writers because they can't cast an actor of the specific intersectionality required.

There has to be some latitude in casting but be aware that this is constantly shifting. As we enter the third decade of the twenty-first century, there is a need for plays with 'non-majority' intersectional characters in them, portrayed by actors with specific ethnicities, races, orientations and gender identities. But for how long?

The important thing is for you, and whoever you are collaborating with, to examine your choices. An actor's history can define their character's identity, and inform how an audience empathizes with what they do. It is not all pretend.

CENSORSHIP

Until 1968, every new play in Britain required a licence from the Lord Chamberlain's Office before it could be publicly performed. The Lord Chamberlain's Office is a department within the British Royal Household. Nowadays it is concerned with matters such as protocol, state visits, investitures, garden parties, the State Opening of Parliament, royal weddings and funerals. Censoring theatre performances, however, was once upon a time part of its remit – a measure initially introduced to protect Prime Minister Robert Walpole's administration from political satire, in 1737.

By the late nineteenth century, the Lord Chamberlain's Office had become the arbiter of moral taste on the stage with general guidelines for withholding performance licences that were never really very clear. There was an attempt to formalize the criteria in 1909, but no legislation followed and the Lord Chamberlain carried on being able to censor whatever he wanted to. Relatively few plays were banned entirely, although Ibsen's *Ghosts* was, and so was Bernard Shaw's *Mrs Warren's Profession*. Many plays had licences delayed (sometimes for long periods) or were passed only after amendments had been made. The British Library holds a file on each and every play, typically containing

Tom Brooke as Gary about to have his teeth hammered out in *Osama the Hero* (2005) by Dennis Kelly.

a reader's report and often extensive correspondence and memoranda, and notes on changes required.

While theatre censorship might not formally exist any more, other aspects of the law have been used by people to try and shut down productions, including charges of blasphemy and indecency. In 2007, a campaigning group called Christian Voice attempted to bring blasphemy charges against the production of *Jerry Springer the Opera* (2006). The show featured tap-dancing Ku Klux Klan members and a nappy-wearing Jesus. The attempt was not successful.

When British Sikh playwright Gurpreet Kaur Bhatti's play *Behzti* (2004) opened in 2004 at the Birmingham Repertory Theatre, a protest was organized by local Sikh leaders because of a controversial rape scene set in a Sikh temple, which was deemed deeply offensive. Violence erupted among the protesters and performances of the play were cancelled two days later. In 2015, writer Omar El-Khairy and director Nadia Latif were tasked with creating a show about the radicalization of young Muslims with members of the National Youth Theatre (NYT). The production was cancelled halfway through the rehearsal period. The artistic director of NYT cited issues with artistic quality; others claimed there were concerns about the radicalism of the piece itself, and who would be influenced by its content. An extract of the play was later performed at an event organized by Index on Censorship, but it has yet to have a full production.

Taboos are not fixed. Society's views about what is permissible on stage are constantly shifting. In the UK, we may no longer have 'big C' Censorship, but censorship with a small 'c' is happening whenever artists and organizations self-censor because they are worried about 'political correctness', igniting any member of the audience's past trauma, what the sponsors of the production might think and whether they are strong enough to face personal attacks from a censorious media.

MARKETING, PRESS AND PUBLICITY

Once your play has been accepted for production, whoever it is that is responsible for marketing it will want to meet with you. In most cases, you will be meeting a team of people, either in-house, employed by the organization on a permanent basis, or from a freelance agency, hired specifically to promote this production. The team might include the Marketing Manager, who will be responsible for the overall marketing campaign, their deputy who will be responsible for print and distribution, including social media, and somebody responsible for dealing with the press and the placing of adverts. This person may also be responsible for collating material for the programme. The team may be joined by a Development Director, who is responsible for talking about the show to potential sponsors and friends of the theatre, the Box Office Manager, responsible for selling tickets, obviously, and the Front of House Manager who may be responsible for the look of the public spaces in the building, and definitely responsible for establishing good relationships with the paying public. The team may vary in size, and the jobs allocated to employees with different titles. It is important, however, for you to understand what everybody is doing to promote your show, so that you can help them.

Before the team start making demands of you, it is worth asking them for their response to your play. Check that they've all read it, understood the story and got the tone. Be prepared for the fact that they may not have done – do not chastise them for this or bear a grudge against them; plays are hard to read. Be prepared to outline the story of your play, who are the main characters and what are the important themes.

They will ask you questions about the play's provenance and your work to date. They should have a copy of your CV but they will want you to write your own 'biog' and give you a set number of words to do it in. They will help decide what achievements to highlight. This biog will not only appear in the programme, but is useful for anybody who has to describe who you are to a potential customer. Don't hide your light under a bushel.

The Press Officer will ask you if you are prepared to do interviews and, if so, with whom and how many. Remember your priority before the show opens is to deal with whatever might emerge from rehearsals. So, however much of a self-publicist you are, don't over-commit yourself.

You may be asked to do a rehearsal blog and to make a contribution to a short trailer that is being made to promote the show.

The Development Director will want to know how prepared you are to meet with potential funders and friends. If you enjoy talking about yourself, your work and eating out, then agree to as many as you can.

The Press Officer may ask you to draft some copy about your show. Take this opportunity to stress what you think is important in what you've written. Find a succinct way of describing the plot without giving it all away. Identify the tone. Don't overdo the adjectives, and don't pretend it is funny when it isn't, particularly. The brochure copy will go through many drafts, as will the press release; make sure you see as many of these as you can without giving the team the impression that you don't think they can do their jobs. Make sure you see the final draft.

The team will ask you for a list of contacts – people you think they should contact to come and see the play. It is very rare that you will have any influence over the ticket pricing strategy for your play, but it is worth finding out. You may be challenged in an interview about them.

The Front of House Manager and the Box Office Manager will ask you about who you think are your target audience, and whether there is anything in your play that some members of the audience might find offensive (e.g. swearing, nudity, violence) and if there is, would you help them to write the 'trigger warning'.

Trigger Warnings

Trigger warnings are attempts to forewarn audiences of content in the play or production that may cause intense physiological and psychological symptoms for people with a variety of anxiety disorders. The tricky thing with trigger warnings is where you draw the line. If a play is built on a series of conflicts and life not turning out right, which many plays are, then there is bound to be material in the play that will upset somebody. Often the point of a play is to explore an upsetting event in order to better understand it and move on.

Some playwrights are concerned that trigger warnings can suggest the outcome of a particular dramatic situation and be a bit of a plot 'spoiler'. Others worry that they can attract 'sensation seekers' – audience members who have a particular fascination with violence or sex or observing characters under extreme duress, with no particular interest in the play itself. Theatre managements do have a duty of care to their audiences, but rather than expecting them to draw attention in their publicity material to everything that could potentially upset an audience member, encourage them to point out that there are scenes in your play that some might find upsetting. If people are worried they should phone the box office for further details. In these litigious times, theatres are concerned that they could be sued by a member of the audience for rekindling the pain of their trauma.

EDUCATION, PARTICIPATION, COMMUNITY

Most theatre-producing organizations, from both the commercial and subsidized sectors, have an individual or team attached to them who is responsible for liaising with schools, local community groups and running a youth theatre and/or a senior citizens' play-reading group. They will expect you to make yourself available to contribute to workshops, participate in any number of question and answer sessions, and pre-and post-show discussions. In any post-show discussion session, make sure there is somebody with you who can chair. Don't ever go into a school on your own. If the company has a young writers' group attached who have been asked to write a short response play to your play, be prepared to read and judge them, if necessary.

EXERCISES

Exercise 1 CV and Biography

- Write a CV.
- Write your biography in 250 words. Research the corporation, production company or theatre that you are applying to and tailor your CV or biography accordingly, matching your interests to theirs.

Exercise 2 Pitching a Play

- Write a short synopsis of the story of your play in 250 words.
- Identify the play's themes and your personal commitment to them.
- Give a brief summary of the structure.
- Write a sentence to describe the tone of your play.

- Write a logline for your play – a single sentence that describes what happens in it. For example, a logline for Macbeth might read: 'Tantalized by a prophecy, a brilliant soldier kills his king to become king himself, but loses his friends, his wife, his kingdom and his mind as a consequence.'
- Identify the play's target audience.

Exercise 3 The Playwright, the Director and the Designer

Describe your ideal relationship with a director and a designer.

Exercise 4 Music and Soundscapes

Choose the music you would want to hear in the production of a play you have written or are writing.

Exercise 5 Trigger Warnings

Identify anything in something you have written that you think might require a 'trigger warning'. Be prepared to say why and then write the wording for the warning.

7
REHEARSAL AND BEYOND

A director interested in new writing must be able to work with the playwright. It is their duty to have involved you in the preproduction process but when it comes to rehearsal, the focus of the director shifts from the playwright and the designer to the actors. The director's medium is the actor in space and time. Space is defined by the stage environment, while time is defined by the duration of each moment, scene, act and the play as a whole. In rehearsals, you are not necessarily the best judge of the dramatic potential of your own script. The director will want you involved in the rehearsal process, indeed you are entitled to be, but not for all of it. They will want you to make changes to the script if bits don't seem to be working or could be improved on, and from time to time, they will want you to massage their ego by telling them what a brilliant job they are doing.

A director's job is a lonely one and it's comforting to have the writer as an ally. At the beginning of the rehearsal process one of the great solaces to a director is the writer being around to share the trials and tribulations of the day, but this doesn't last for long. Negotiate what your role is going to be before rehearsals start.

In the rehearsal room, actors don't like to feel that they are being directed by more than one person. Don't ever try and note an actor without the director's permission. It is crucial that you agree with the director a time when you can ask questions about what you have witnessed in rehearsals and to make your suggestions. Inexperienced writers are often surprised at the pace at which things move in rehearsal – the time spent discussing and trying out options, when to the playwright it is perfectly obvious what is intended. It may seem a complete waste of time to you, but actors need to be convinced by their character choices, and this only happens if they have tried various options.

In order for a production to sustain any sort of run of performances, the foundations of the production have to be strong; the choices understood and committed to. In rehearsal, the foundations are laid by the director and the actors, through trial and error. If the possibilities of the writing aren't rigorously explored in rehearsal, there is a danger that the actors will start experimenting with your text in performance and the meaning and impact of your play could be totally skewed. You and the director may have gone through your script with a fine tooth comb, but it is surprising how much more is revealed, and how many more questions need answering, when the actors get hold of it.

It is common for the director to ask you to be present at the first read-through and as they work through the script with the acting company for the first time. This can take a week to ten days, of an average four-week rehearsal period. You need to be part of this process. Be prepared to answer questions from anyone, however obvious the answer. Don't preface your answer by raising your eyebrows or clicking your tongue. Don't feel bad if you can't answer a question. Just as a good director should not be afraid to appear stupid in front of the actors, neither should you. The rehearsal process is a process of discovery for all involved. It is a safe space. It is the director's job to make sure no one is ignored and that their contribution is valued.

Having worked through the script in detail with you and the actors, most directors will then expect you to leave rehearsals for a while, so that they can get on with discovering the play without you. It is sometimes hard to leave the 'party' at this stage, but crucial that you do. At the end of the day, you are handing over ownership of your play to the actors to make of it what they will.

In the same way that actors don't like directors who act out their parts as a way of trying to get them to do something, directors and actors don't want the writer breathing down their necks the whole time saying 'No, it doesn't mean that, it means this!' or 'Is she really going to do it like that?'

and so on, as they experiment with your text to find what works for them. The director may call on you at any stage in the next two weeks to have a look at a scene or scenes, if they feel they need attention. It is best to be away for as long as you can, so that when you return, you will be a fresh pair of eyes on proceedings and you can delight in, or be shocked by, what the actors have achieved.

If being away from the rehearsal room makes you feel anxious, you can always phone the director or set up a regular time to speak with their assistant or dramaturg, should they have either or both. If the director doesn't mind, they may let you talk to the Deputy Stage Manager who sits in on every rehearsal marking a script with every move the actors make, and where the director would like to put sound and lighting cues. This Deputy Stage Manager's script is known as the 'the production script', or 'the book'.

Joseph Mydell and Sidney Cole in *Master Harold and the Boys* (1982) by Athol Fugard, at the Contact Theatre Manchester 1989. The play takes place in South Africa during the apartheid era.

The First Day

Most rehearsal processes will start with what is called 'a meet and greet'. The purpose of a meet and greet is twofold: it is an opportunity to put names to faces, and for people who are not going to be in the rehearsal room to learn about the production. There is no more nerve-wracking day for all those involved in the rehearsal process than the first day. (Well, perhaps the first time in front of an audience, or the press night. But that depends on how confident people are feeling about what they have created in rehearsal.)

On the morning of the first day, a group of strangers, some of whom you will have already met (actors, the production manager, some of the management staff), others you might not have done (the stage-management team, any assistants and more of the organization's staff), gather together 'to do' your play. The producer, or chief executive of the company, who may be the artistic director, will call the room to order, ask everyone to form one large circle, welcome everybody and give a short introduction to the mission of the theatre, where the play fits within the season and how pleased they are to be doing it, and so should everybody in the room be pleased and excited. Then it is expected that everyone in the circle announces their name, their job title and gives a short description of what they do. You can't be expected to remember who everybody is, but it is assumed that were you to bump into any of the circle in the corridor, or at lunch, you'd feel confident enough to reintroduce yourself, or at the very least acknowledge them. Introductions over, half the room will leave, and the other half stay for a presentation of the designer's model box and costume drawings. This is done by the designer/s and the director.

At this stage, you may be asked to give an introduction to your play. If so, keep it short. Talk a little bit about the history of how you came to write it. Give a brief synopsis of the story and what are the important themes, and how thrilled you are to have such a talented group of people working on it. At the end of the design model box presentation, the assembled group will be asked if they have any questions about the play, the set and costumes. The actors may have a few, and if you haven't seen the final design in the model box, this is your chance to comment on it. Whatever you do though, do not undermine the presentation of the designer and director if they have started to talk about your play in a way that you don't understand, or there are additions to the design you hadn't anticipated. If you have been surprised by what you have seen and heard in the course of the first day, challenge the director and designer at a later stage, privately. For the creative team to appear to be singing from the same hymn sheet is all-important, because right from the start, the rehearsal process should be about building an actors' confidence with the play and all the elements of the production.

Once this presentation is over, a few more people will leave and the only people now in the room should be the actors who are going to be involved in the read-through, and those the director is prepared to let listen to it. This will usually involve members of the marketing and education/participation departments.

Some directors and actors are unnecessarily coy about first read-throughs. It is true that it's the first time the actors will read the play together, and they will be making judgements about the standard of each other's reading, but no one is expecting anyone to give their final performance at the read-through. Very, very few actors' performances don't grow in complexity and sensitivity through the rehearsal period.

If there is going to be an audience of any sort at the first read-through – there always will be, even if it's only you – ask the director to make sure the actors 'go for it'. This could be the very first time you hear your whole play read out loud. You want to get a real sense of what the actors can deliver as a group. It is hard to see what is to be gained by asking the actors to read a play 'neutrally'. It is even harder to see what the point is of doing a read-through with the actors not reading their own parts. This can be a useful exercise later in the rehearsal process, if the director feels that the actors aren't listening to whom they are talking.

After a successful read-through, a general discussion is had with the company about the play – the characters, the themes, the relevance and so on. If you are asked questions, be honest in your answers. If you know nothing about the characters other than what they are doing in your play, say so. Let the actors know that, as far as you are concerned, everything they need to know is in the play, but if they want to invent additional reasons for their actions that will not distract but enrich our experience of what they're doing, then that's fine by you.

If actors, who may have been mulling over your lines for a few days, ask you to start changing lines, then in the politest possible way, thank them, appear to make a note of what they have said and let them know that you will think about it, but that you will have to discuss any changes with the director before getting back to them. Look out for phrases like: 'I'm not sure my character would say this', 'Would you mind if I cut the following line', 'I'm not sure that would have been the way they would have expressed that back then'.

No two actors will have been trained in the same way and what is important in the early stages of rehearsal is for the director to build the 'ensemble'. Directors choose different ways to do this. Some will start with exercises, games and improvisations, and others will start with tablework. As long as the instructions for the games and improvisations are clear, and everybody knows the purpose of what they are doing, this can be a fun way to start. You may even be asked to participate.

'Tablework' to build a collective understanding of the play is a far more common way of building an ensemble, especially amongst more experienced directors.

Tablework

Tablework is text work: dividing the play into manageable sections, often defined by subject matter, and analysing the text in each section in detail,

around a table. Tablework should also involve sharing research – discussing the world at the time the writer wrote the play, the world of the play and where these two worlds connect to the contemporary world.

Some directors will, as part of this tablework, want to do the actors' job with them and identify each character's thought, as a unit. This gives a further structure to the early days of rehearsal. They'll want to discuss what it is the character wants in each unit, and the manner in which they are trying to get what they want. They will attempt to identify a transitive verb that doesn't describe a character's state of being, but what the character is doing to the character they are speaking to, when they say the line. This is called 'actioning'. For example, if my objective is to make you fall in love with me, I may try many different strategies to achieve this. Within one speech, on different lines, I may flatter you, I may impress you, I might enchant you and so on.

Some actors like to prioritize intellectual analysis over instinct, and actioning gives them a real sense of having spent the day working. For others it is a waste of time. They find it difficult it come up with transitive verbs and will argue that until they have had the opportunity to play with the text on their feet, they don't know what they're doing to the other character, and anyway whatever they think they're doing in the early stages of rehearsal, it's bound to change. These actors often end up inventing words to describe their actions, which can be a lot of fun, but difficult to play.

If, as a playwright, you are interested in trying to understand the creative process by which some actors find their characters, 'actioning' can be a fascinating process to watch. It can inform your writing.

Active Analysis

There is an approach, however, that is much more exhilarating, and is somewhere between sitting around a table and getting up and doing the scene.

It's called 'active analysis'. It is a late development of the Stanislavsky system. The Stanislavsky system is a series of acting techniques, based on emotional memory and inner impulses, to ensure a certain high standard of acting. Great acting, Konstantin Stanislavsky (1863–1938) always believed, could only be achieved if the actors subordinated themselves to the demands of the play.

In the last four years of his life, when Stalin took control of the Soviet Union, Stanislavsky was confined to his home and was not allowed to set foot in a theatre. The newspapers told the world he was too old and too sick but in fact he was working at home with a select group of actors on what has become known as active analysis. Through active analysis, actors explore the text through improvisation, to discover the need for their lines. They are working a flexible, spontaneous, imaginative muscle as they grow to inhabit the text. The process is simple. The actors read a section of the text, they talk about it – who does what and why and in what order – and then they get up and improvise what they've read. They then return to the table, read the text again and talk about what they have added to, or left out of, the text. They read the text again and then repeat the exercise. They do this until the actors discover the lines the playwright has written. It is an extraordinary process to witness.

What an Actor Offers

Once, when asked by an artistic director to rehearse three new plays back to back, I didn't immediately accept the offer. I didn't relish the prospect because, in my experience, an actor's approach to working on a new play is very different to the approach they would have working on a classic. They bring less of their imagination to the rehearsal process and are more inhibited in their choices, preferring always to defer to the playwright, as if they owned the key to a definitive production. The playwrights I was working with at the time were all inexperienced and hadn't a clue about the amazing amount an actor could bring to their scripts.

I agreed to do the job once I had decided that the only way to overcome my frustration would be to see if I could get an agreement at the beginning of the process from the actors as to what they thought acting was all about, and what they were prepared to bring to the rehearsal process.

Regardless of the fact that the whole company had trained at different acting schools, they agreed they all had a responsibility, using whatever individual process they had learnt, to embody character, to transform and play someone other than themselves. They all agreed to call this activity 'embodying'. They then also agreed that the choices they would make about a character, and their role in the scene, would inevitably be affected by their own politics, and by whatever was going on in the contemporary world. They agreed that performances and productions are not set in aspic because they are inevitably nuanced by the mindset of the audience, with whom the actors are sharing the same space. Therefore, they agreed to explore the politics of their choices more rigorously than we had in other rehearsal processes and to find overt ways to share their choices with the audience. This they called 'dressing'. They were 'dressing' the part with comment. Finally, they agreed that actors didn't always have to act 'in character' but could work as a physical or vocal chorus to facilitate the narrative or enhance the emotional impact of a scene in an expressionistic way. This they called 'leotarding'. 'Leotarding' because at the time certain types of abstract physical theatrical presentations were very much in fashion, and the performers in them were rarely identified individually and often appeared to be wearing a leotard uniform.

Back to Rehearsals

After a couple of weeks you, the playwright, return to the rehearsal room to see a few scenes, or a stagger through of Part One or even a rough run of the whole play, and you will be amazed by the progress that has been made.

When you see a scene on its feet, and you realize the reason it's not working is nothing to do with the actors but something to do with the writing – rewrite it! Inevitably, at this stage there will be things that need expanding and excising in the script.

Again, if an actor starts asking you to rewrite lines or cut them, because they can't make them work for whatever reason, don't oblige too readily. Remember, you have been living with your characters a lot longer than they have, and it is an actor's job to make your lines work. To keep the peace, the director might ask the actor to put brackets around the line rather than cut it. If, after four weeks or however long the rehearsal period is, the actor still can't find a way to say the line persuasively, and doesn't feel the need to say it, it may have to be cut or rewritten for that particular production. Stick, however, with what you intended for the published edition. Should your play be produced more than once, you may find the next actor playing the part won't have a problem with the line and you will wonder what all the fuss was about.

The Director in Rehearsal

No two directors will work in the same way. If you work with the same director twice, don't be surprised if they approach your second collaboration in a completely different way. There is no standard director's training in the UK. Regardless of how the director has become a director, it is agreed in the profession that they are responsible for supervising rehearsals, explaining the ideas behind the production, critiquing performances and making suggestions for improvements. They also assume the role of the ideal audience.

Each moment of the performance may be thought of as a picture capable of communicating with the audience semiotically. In creating the stage picture, the director will emphasize significant elements and subordinate others. This is done through the positioning of the actors in the space. For example, an actor facing the audience is more dominant than one with their back to us, one standing up more dominant than the one sitting, unless they are sitting on a throne in the centre of the stage, of course. There are specific stage areas with more significance than others determined by our culture – a culture that sees symmetry as essential to beauty and reads from left to right. Different cultures read colour in different ways and directors have to be sensitive to this too. A director is responsible for focusing the attention of the audience, making sure that they see and hear what the director wants them to see and hear. This can be assisted not only by the composition of the stage picture, but by careful lighting and clever use of sound.

Aside from words like motivation, objective and action, which are used to describe what an actor is doing, there is a vocabulary specific to the rehearsal room, which can at first feel like a foreign language. Here are some of the words you might encounter and what they mean:

- **Blocking.** This is the word used when a director chooses to tell an actor where to stand and when to move, before they have had a chance to find the reason 'why'. Blocking is considered non-*de rigueur* in the professional theatre, but essential in amateur theatre, when the actors aren't rehearsing all day. In the professional theatre, it is assumed that when the actor knows what they are doing in a scene, they will be able to position themselves correctly in the scene... with a little bit of help from the director!

- **Pacing.** When directors and actors talk about altering the pace of a production, they are not simply talking about asking actors to speed up or slow down the delivery of the lines (more often than not the former) but asking them to look again at the stakes in any particular scene, and 'up' them.

- **Business.** 'Stage business' is an incidental activity performed by the actor to enhance the drama, but it can easily detract from what is being said. For example, if the actor playing The Second Murderer in *Macbeth* spent the whole scene trying to catch a fly whilst Macbeth was giving him instructions to murder Macduff, this bit of stage business, because it is not supported by the text, might be considered unnecessary. If, on the other hand, the choreographed swatting were to complement the changes in thought within the scene and give us some insight into the character of the Murderer, this could be brilliant business. A production choice.

- **A run.** A run is doing the whole play in the rehearsal room.
- **A stagger through.** This is a hesitant run of the play, more of a lurch, where the time it takes is not the main concern. It is about checking that everybody knows the running order of the scenes, their lines, where to move, and where to enter and exit.
- **Tech rehearsals/teching.** These are rehearsals on stage when the actors get a chance to walk the set, practise their entrances and exits, see the lights and hear any soundscape, for the first time. At this stage, lighting and sound cues are plotted into 'the book'. Techs take an enormously long time. For the writer to sit in an empty auditorium unable to influence anything that is going on onstage is worse than watching paint dry.
- **Dress rehearsal.** A dress rehearsal is when all the elements of the production come together. The first dress rehearsal usually comes at the end of a long day or two of 'teching' and can be agonizing for the playwright. Suddenly, no one seems to know what they're saying, your lines don't make any sense and your play, which was supposed to last one and a half hours, is running at nearly three. You want to curse the director and wish you had never offered it to them or, better still, never written the play. Don't fret, things do improve in the second dress rehearsal and over previews, as the actors become more familiar with the technical requirements of the space, and they rediscover and build on the performances they discovered in the rehearsal room.

- **Previews.** These are performances in front of a paying public before the production is shown to the press. You may get two or three, or many more, depending on how long your play is expected to run. Be expected to fine-tune your script or, in some cases, to make radical changes, as you are required to acknowledge and respond to audience reactions. Be wary of inviting friends and family to previews. Their supportive, or not so supportive, comments can totally undermine your relationship with the director.
- **Cuts.** An audience's attention span for a serious play seems to vary from year to year. Some people say that if the play is good enough, and the production awe-inspiring, it doesn't matter how long it is, but for most theatre managements, it does. Whether that's because they want to make sure the audience can get home before public transport stops, or they want to avoid having to pay their front of house staff overtime, or simply because they want to earn from people buying drinks after the show, two and a half hours running time, including the interval, seems nowadays to be the limit. That's with a 7.30pm or 8pm start.

If in the last quarter of your rehearsal period, when the actors have learnt their parts and they are running your play, it appears to be running far too long, it is important to cut it. The 'runs' of plays do speed up towards the end of the rehearsal process and in previews, but not by that much! The later you leave cutting your play, the more disruptive it can be to the build-up to the first night in front of an audience.

You must be allowed to decide on the criteria for the cuts with the director and then do them. It is important to decide on the criteria, because the chances are you will have to lose some of your favourite lines. To avoid a lengthy, and potentially torturous, session with the director, cut your scripts separately and then bring the two together. With any luck, if you have agreed the criteria, you will find that you and the director concur on most cuts, and there shouldn't be too much left to argue about. Whatever cuts you make, directors will always want to ensure the story is clear, and you should too. When the cuts are given to the actors, it is important for you and the director to stand your ground. If you don't, it doesn't take long for a group of actors to argue the case to have half the cuts reinstated, and you'll have to repeat the whole exercise again.

- **The press night.** This is the night that the press come to see your play. The number of critics who turn up will depend on who is in it, where it is being put on, what it's about and who you are. It will rarely depend on the director or who's producing. Members of the company are allocated a number of complimentary tickets (comps) on press night – usually two. Don't expect to be offered any more than any other member of the company, just because you've written it. The performance is often followed by a party, where everyone hugs, gushes 'thanks' to each other and gets drunk. Putting on a play can be an intense and stressful process, and people need to unwind and celebrate their considerable achievement.

It is probably every writer's dream to develop a long-term relationship with a director who they can trust. The reality of the situation, however, is that the theatre industry is subject to the vagaries of fashion and the chances of both your careers being in step with each other isn't very likely.

Make the most of each rehearsal situation, and don't be too anxious about whether they are rehearsing your play properly. If you are invited to attend rehearsals and you happen to be in a bad mood, for whatever reason, leave the mood behind as you enter the room. Look interested, even if you are bored by what's going on and, most importantly, don't comment unless you are invited to.

HOW TO DEAL WITH REVIEWS

The good ones you forget, the bad ones stay with you forever. The passage of time may ease some of the pain, but it never disappears entirely.

One way to avoid the pain is not to read your reviews. It is, however, impossible to avoid their impact entirely. You will feel it off the actors, staff and audiences when you walk into the theatre the next time you come and watch the show. The atmosphere will be completely different, depending on whether the production of your play has had good or bad reviews.

If you do read your reviews, check with the director whether the actors have read them before you go to congratulate them or commiserate with them. A lot of actors don't read reviews, good or bad, because of the effect it can have on their performance – especially if they have been cited personally.

With so many opportunities on social media and in the press for critics to express an opinion about your work, you will inevitably get some good reviews and some 'stinkers', although smaller productions in less prestigious venues don't get the plethora of reviewers that turn up to some larger theatres.

Unfortunately, the democratization of reviews these days has meant that very few critics have the subject knowledge, history and critical context to actually analyse and contextualize a play. Most of them only know how to write in attention-seeking soundbites. Their reviews often say more about them than about what they have been to review. Their reviews are often inaccurate, cruel and personal. The advice used to be – don't ever respond to a good or bad review by writing back to the critic. But if someone is judging you in public, there is no reason not to comment on their judgement, as long as you are prepared for the consequences. Don't be a coward – do it under your own name and make sure to thank the critic for anything they have had to say that has made you think about your work going forward. You can learn from a good critic, even if they don't like your play.

When your reviews come out, don't ever expect too much sympathy or overt praise from your theatre contemporaries, particularly your writer friends. The theatre is a competitive business, and your friends will enjoy a bit of 'schadenfreude' just as much as you do.

The business of the critics giving shows star ratings is fine when they are in your favour, and deeply humiliating when not. It is often unclear whether it is the reviewer who has awarded the stars, or the arts' editor on the basis of the review. Either way, everything gets far too many stars for it to really mean anything. Perhaps if you share the taste of the critic, the 'stars' can be a helpful stamp of approval and a guide to whether you are going to enjoy the experience if you go and see the play. There are many better reasons to go and see a show, other than by counting the number of stars it has garnered.

Remember, the response to all art is subjective. There is never one right answer, just one you can live with. Let Oscar Wilde have the final word on the matter: 'Critics have often spoiled my breakfast, but never my lunch.'

SECOND PRODUCTIONS

Much to the frustration of most playwrights, it can take years for a play to get a second production. There are a number of reasons for this:

- The first production may not have been reviewed well, if at all.
- The first production may have happened as a result of a commitment to new writing from your local theatre, and your connection with them.
- Your play may have won a content- or form-specific playwriting competition.
- The subject matter may have lost its currency.
- The play text may not be easily accessible if it hasn't been published.
- Your agent may not have the will or the knowledge to know where to send it.
- A production slot in a season is competing with unproduced work and any play ever written that takes the company's fancy.

If you are lucky enough to get a second production shortly after the first, it is an excellent opportunity to revisit your script and make it better. Don't give up hope though that one day a director or producer will turn to your play. The vast majority of plays that are produced have been produced before.

8
THE PROFESSIONAL PLAYWRIGHT

DIRECTING YOUR OWN WORK

A professional playwright is a writer who gets paid for their writing. In order to do this, you have to find people who are committed to presenting your play and have the resources to put it on, and to pay you, a production team and actors.

Playwrights might seem to be the natural choice to direct their own work, especially if the stories they want to tell are based on their own experiences, but unless you know something of the craft of directing, you'd be ill advised to do so. Why? You may know exactly what you want to see on stage and hear the tune of what you have written, but unless you have the diplomatic and imaginative skills to encourage the actors to find and create and add to your vision, for themselves, you are likely to remain frustrated. The theatre, as has been said many times, is a collaborative art form, and if you have to resort to acting out the part for the actor and giving them line readings to get them to say the line in the way you want it said, then you are not directing.

The most admired and successful playwrights who have directed their own work include Shakespeare, Molière, Brecht, Eduardo Fillipo, Edward Albee, Harold Pinter, Sam Shepherd and Dario Fo, to more contemporary writers like Peter Gill, David Mamet, David Hare, Alan Ayckbourn, Nina Raine, John Godber, Antony Nielsen and Robert Icke. It is important to know that they have all had experience either as actors or assistant directors or both before venturing into directing their own material.

It is possible to do more than one job in the theatre well, as long as you understand that the jobs are different and that they require different skills that need to be learned and practised. You've got to know something about directing and how to animate your text before attempting to direct it.

There is always a case to let playwrights, who are energetic and good communicators with an original, revelatory, theatrical imagination, direct the first production of their own play. Their entire individual vision is what will inspire their collaborators and will be what the audience wants to see on stage. Emma Rice, artistic director of Wise Children, is one such writer/director.

For the most part, however, playwrights generally are not necessarily the best judge of what they've written. A good director will see things in the writing that you didn't know were there and will find something particular to themselves in your script. The playwright is like the first runner in a relay race. Having done your lap, it's now time to hand over to someone else.

OPPOSITE: Scott Lyons and Stephen Bloomer in a writing class.

Ben Elton, in *IVAN* (1979), an adaptation of Tolstoy's *The Death of Ivan Ilyich* by Anthony Clark

SELF-PRODUCING

One route to getting your work on, and perhaps the most challenging, is to self-produce. It involves a lot of time and effort, and you need to know why you are doing it. If the only reason why you are doing it is because no one else will do your play, then check if you've exhausted every possible outlet, and reread any feedback you've had. Perhaps your play isn't ready yet or its subject matter doesn't chime with the zeitgeist.

If, on reflection, you still strongly believe that people have missed how brilliant your play is and you want to prove it to them, and you want to self-produce in order to build your career through getting reviews and having a professional credit, and you want to develop your craft by exposing the work to an audience, then okay, fine, go ahead.

Self-producing is not to be recommended unless you are a good communicator, resourceful, enjoy solving problems and are convinced that you can find an audience for the work. You will need to learn how to budget your production, raise the money for it, from both the private and public sectors, find a venue, a director, a designer and a cast, and decide for how long you are going to run the play, and how you are going to sell it. The producing process can take up to a couple of years, so you need to be patient, persistent and plan well.

A good producer, if they lose money on a production, doesn't lose their own money. Most first-time writers and directors who self-produce unfortunately do – and their losses can be considerable.

Many writers who self-produce start by setting up a company with some of their contemporaries. Choosing a name for the company can be fun, but then you've got to sort out its mission and its artistic policy. Your mission is why the company exists and the artistic policy is what you do to realize your mission. There are very few writer-led companies, but there is no reason why there shouldn't be more. Information about how to set up a not-for-profit company, limited by guarantee, is available on the Independent Theatre Council website. Once you have set up an independent company, part of the job of the producer is to look for other companies who share your company's ethos, to co-produce with. Start with your local, state-subsidized company, who should give priority to the work of artists in their region.

PITCHING

Playwrights rarely pitch to sell their scripts and ideas in the way that screenwriters do. If you are asked to a meeting by an artistic director, literary manager or dramaturg, because they are interested in commissioning a play from you or they would like to work with your company, make sure that you prepare what you are going to say. You want to be able to control the meeting and sell yourself persuasively. Here is an *aide-mémoire* using the letters in MY STRATEGY to prompt what you should talk about.

M = ME

Give a short biography of yourself, emphasizing your achievements.

Y = YOU

Let the person you are talking to know that you know something about the theatre they are working in. If they are a director, talk about a play you have seen that they have directed. Between being asked to attend a meeting and having the meeting, find out as much as you can about the person you are seeing and where they work.

S = STORY

Outline the story of your play as succinctly as you can. Prepare by writing a synopsis before-hand, which you should keep editing and rehearsing until you have got it as clear and as short as possible. It may not be necessary to tell the whole story. Focus on the essential elements and let them know from whose perspective the story is being told.

T = THEMES

Identify the main themes you are writing about, and how they emerge through the story.

R = RELEVANCE

Describe the contemporary relevance of your themes.

A = AUDIENCE

Pinpoint your target audience for the play without, of course, discriminating against other constituencies that the theatre may want to attract to see it.

T = TONE

Let them know the tone of your play.

E = EXPENSE

Make them aware of the cast size and any special technical requirements the production of the play might need. Hint at the number of locations you are intending to write for, or you have written for.

G = GENRE and GOOD

If you are writing within a particular genre, identify how you are using its familiar tropes. If you are not writing within a genre, choose one or two features of the play that you are particularly proud of – that you think are good: powerful story, complex characters, unpredictable dialogue and so on.

Y = YES

Sum up what you have said, making it very clear why you think they should say 'yes'! 'Yes' we'll commission you or 'Yes' we'll programme that play.

Throughout your pitch it is important that you are enthusiastic about your own work. Don't appear too self-effacing or too arrogant. Make sure that you have sold the emotional content of what you have written.

COVER LETTER

A cover letter is a letter of between 250 and 400 words that introduces you and your play to the recipient. It accompanies your script. In your first

Chipo Chung and Alex Hassell in *Turandot* (1953) in new version by Edward Kemp (2008), Premiered at Hampstead Theatre.

paragraph, explain who you are and grab the reader's attention with your top three achievements. Don't give a full résumé. In your second paragraph, explain why you are sending them your play, highlighting elements of writing that you think will appeal to them. Don't attempt a synopsis of the story. A sentence about the story, the characters, the style and who you want to reach with the work is all you need. In a final paragraph, explain why you think your play is a must for their company. Make sure your letter is well formatted.

PLAYWRIGHTS CAN RARELY LIVE BY STAGE PLAYS ALONE

Unless you are incredibly lucky, and prolific, you will not be able to live off your earnings writing for the stage. If you are serious about having a career as a playwright, you need to subsidize your income in other ways. You may want to learn to write for other media as well as the stage.

Writing for Audio – Podcasts and Radio

An audio play, once known as a radio play, can be defined quite simply as a story told in dramatic form by means of sound alone. These are usually pre-recorded and listened to live on the radio, or on demand as a podcast. It is a bit of a generalization, but for people who grew up without the internet or social media, live radio is still the convenient way for them to consume audio content. For the tech-savvy Millennials who want to consume media on their terms, podcasts, which you can listen and relisten to when you want, are more accessible. Although most radio content is now available on demand, there is still a sense that radio deals with what is newsworthy and current, and podcasting is primarily a niche-based medium. Radio does still produce narrative drama, but within a strict format. Podcasters are not under the same regulations as radio producers. Podcasts are unhindered by radio station format, time constraints and subject matter. People who like audio will listen to both the radio and podcasts.

Many playwrights first gained a public for their work through writing for audio and still do. The good audio writer stimulates, through their choice of words and sounds, the listener to imagine the period when the play is set, what the characters look like, where they are, what they are doing, what is happening to them and, crucially, what they are thinking about and the speed at which they think. To make sure that your play keeps the audience listening, find a strong narrative with themes that are relevant. Although audio is an intimate medium and lends itself to the use of a narrator, don't rely on this entirely, if at all. An audio play is not an audio book. Structure your play, as you would a stage play, through a series of conflicts that build to a climax that is then resolved or not. Don't write for too many voices.

If you are writing for radio, familiarize yourself with any commissioning guidelines the broadcaster has. When listening to the radio or podcasts make a note of the producer's name, because most submissions for commission have to come with a producer attached. Unless the company is trawling for writers by inviting them to submit unsolicited material, you will need to send your work to a producer. Write to the producer via the company that has produced the work or track their contact details down online. If the producer has an agent, then send it to the agent for the attention of that person.

Script readers and producers are better disposed towards professionally presented scripts. Type all directions and sound effects in capital letters.

Writing for Film and/or TV

We live in a film- and TV-dominated culture and there is a wealth of good writing for both. It is hard to be definitive about this, because there are so many exceptions, but film scripts, like a lot of plays, tend to focus on a strong central character with clearly defined needs and obstacles to those needs. In film, the stories are told primarily through action and visuals, and have a clear beginning, middle and end, and respect a five-act structure. The locations tend to be expansive and exotic. The themes reach out to the viewer's humanity.

In TV, the story is told primarily through dialogue, although visuals and action are still important – more important than they are in a stage play. TV stories are episodic and allow for multiple beginnings, middles and ends. Each episode is part of a larger narrative. The stories often involve a group of characters with a range of different problems, each with their own character arc divided across a number of episodes. Their problems can seem petty when compared to those of a feature film protagonist.

Both TV and film scripts look the same on the page, both are typed up using screenwriting software and both use location headings, character headings, scene descriptions and dialogue. Most TV episodes are either thirty or sixty minutes, with commercial breaks, while feature films are at least ninety minutes. That said, programming patterns are constantly changing, as more and more producing companies are competing for viewing figures with work that is either streamed or available on demand. Before attempting a screenplay, it is worth having an idea where you would like to place it.

Even if you are primarily planning to write for the stage, it is worth having what is known as a spec script – an unsolicited non-commissioned screenplay – in your portfolio, which shows how you can tell a story through action. A good literary agent is invariably going to want to put you forward for screen work because it pays so much better than the stage. A lot of successful writers for film and TV started their careers writing for the stage.

WRITING WITH OTHERS

If you're going to write with somebody else, it goes without saying that you should choose somebody whose work you respect. Writing with somebody else offers challenges and pleasures in equal measure. On the negative side, you may not agree with each other's ideas or on what direction the play should take. You may start to resent the fact that you seem to be working much harder than your writing partner. Editing can suddenly become a nightmare if the lion's share of what is being cut are the lines that you wrote. On the plus side, though, writing with somebody else can speed up the process. Two minds exploring ideas from different points of view and inventing complex characters and unpredictable story lines to reveal the themes that you both feel passionate about can be a lot of fun. Bouncing ideas off each other can take your writing to unexpected places. Writing can be a lonely, daunting process and sharing the job with somebody else can make it less so.

If you are going to write with somebody else, be sure to agree on what you're going to write about before you start, and what form you think it should take. Set up some practical ground rules. Are you going to write everything together? Or are you, having agreed an outline, going to allocate each other specific scenes and come back to share them? Are you going to write in the same space? Or are you going to write separately, and edit each other's contributions? If so, agree that you are not allowed to undo each other's edits. How often are you going to meet? Having agreed on a synopsis, are you each going to write different scenes? Or choose different characters and improvise the dialogue together? Agree on a writer's clock and set yourself deadlines. Each partnership is different and will need to be set in its own unique way. The better you plan the collaboration, the more fun you will have and the more you will achieve.

It is very important to take the time, before you start writing together, to draw up a collaboration agreement, like a prenuptial agreement, and put it in writing. This will avoid any arguments about copyright, credits and payments further down the line.

Team Writing

Team writing is not unheard of in the theatre but it is very rare. You are more likely to come across it in TV, where there is pressure is to produce a number of episodes of a show. Team writing is when you start work on an idea or story in a room with a team of writers. Maybe up to six, maybe fewer, maybe more… Together you thrash around the subject and come up with an outline narrative. Collectively, you add detail to this outline before you separate to write your own bit. When you've done your bit, you submit it to the group and receive notes from all of them. These, you hope, will inspire you to develop what you have written.

The Writer in the Devising Process

Devising companies work with writers in a number of different ways, depending on their practise. The most common is that a freelance playwright is employed specifically to research a subject and to develop a script in collaboration with the company, which might include a director, a designer, a composer, a choreographer and actors. The role of the playwright in a devising process is different from that of the conventional playwright, who is considered the initiator and author of a script, because they will be expected to incorporate the ideas and research of others and be expected to take advantage of the palette of performance skills the company is offering.

If you are employed by a devising company, be very clear what role you are going to play in this process and what the contractual arrangements are when it comes to who has the right to claim authorship of the finished script. Often problems of authorship don't arise until a script is published, when the devisers of the script have not been asked permission to use what they consider their material, and they haven't been offered any financial remuneration. In the UK, the Writers' Guild of Great Britain supports the belief that whoever scripts the material within the group is the author, regardless of how that material was generated.

Playwrights who work with devising companies on a regular basis will say that many of the characters and scenes in their finished play will have been based on ideas that have come from improvisations, but the play itself is not improvised. It is a written text and the actors did not make up all the lines.

In the same way that playwrights can enjoy working with another writer or in a team, so working with a devising company offers a creative environment in which you can learn a lot, in which ideas about content and form are interrogated, and experiment is the name of the game.

Be clear with the company how you want to receive feedback on drafts of the script. If everybody wants to have an input, then the company needs to appoint a chairperson to collect everyone's comments and organize them into a coherent piece of feedback that identifies what is good about what you have written and where they think there is room for improvement.

A devising company may employ a playwright more as dramaturg than someone who writes dialogue for particular scenes. In this case, the playwright will be asked to organize and edit material to identify themes, events, character arcs, symbols and so on; in short, to write a scenario, to give dramatic shape to the material. They may ask you to contribute a series of written pieces that they can use as stimulus texts for their improvisations.

Collective Writing

You may be interested in working with a devising company on a piece of 'collective writing' – a piece of writing where anybody's views on any aspect of the process are as valid as anybody else's. So, anybody can write, act and direct. A group devising and writing collectively needs a lot of time to work things through, and even then, the likelihood is that the play will suffer from a lack of cohesive style and a clear vision.

If you, as the playwright, are asked to set up an improvisation, or you feel that something is missing from a particular scene and want the actors to improvise it to find a solution, then it is very important to be clear with your instructions. You don't want to be prescriptive but you don't want the improvisation to lose its focus. Clarify the characters' 'wants' and/or 'needs' for the actors, perhaps identify the obstacle or obstacles to them getting what they want and see how the actors resolve the situation. Alternatively, if you know the ending but don't know how to get there, see if the actors can identify the obstacles and how the characters overcome them.

EXERCISES

Exercise 1 Placing a Play

Choose a play you know well and a theatre you think should programme that play and write a letter to their artistic director.

Exercise 2 Writing for Different Media

Find a scene that you have written for the stage. Write the same scene for two other media, e.g. audio and film. Notice the differences. How much do they vary in length and why?

Exercise 3 Co-writing

Find a writer with whom you are compatible and write a short story together on no more than one side of A4. Decide whose perspective you are going to tell the story from and plot a scenario together. Then write the dialogue. Rewrite the scene a number of times, without undoing each other's edits.

Exercise 4 Improvisation to the Rescue

Working with actors, or acting students, lead an improvisation to inform your writing.

- *Write a scene for two or three characters that sets up a situation that you can't resolve. Let the actors' improvisation give you the ending.*
- *Give the actors the last line of your scene and let them find the beginning.*
- *Write a list of five important things that might happen in your short five-scene play. You are not sure of the order in which the things will happen, but they do occur, and the play has a beginning, middle and end. Give two to three actors a brief character description. Get them to improvise the first scene. Ring a bell when you think they have reached the end of the first scene. Swap the parts amongst the actors and get them to improvise the second scene. Continue the improvisation, swapping parts in each scene until you have completed scene five. Film/record the improvisation.*

9
MORE OPPORTUNITIES

Given the amount of time it takes to write an original stage play, the opportunities available to you to have it produced, and the amount of money you are likely to earn from it (unless you are extremely lucky), it is important to be prepared to consider adaptation work, writing for different media and writing with a co-writer or as part of a team of writers.

ADAPTATION

Nearly 50 per cent of all films made are based on novels. Over 90 per cent of all musicals are adaptations of novels or plays. Theatres have been adapting books since time immemorial. It is very rare not to see at least one adaptation in a theatre's programme in the course of a year. Usually the adaptation is of a set text (a text being studied for a school examination) or a popular nineteenth- or twentieth-century classic novel, e.g. *Jane Eyre* (1847) by Charlotte Bronte or *Hard Times* (1854) by Charles Dickens, or a fairy tale, e.g. *Cinderella* or *The Snow Queen*, or a piece of contemporary children's literature, e.g. *War Horse* (1982) by Michael Morpurgo or *Gangster Granny* (2011) by David Walliams. Sometimes a classical film will be adapted for the stage, e.g. *Billy Elliot* (2000) by Lee Hall, *The Graduate* (1967) by Buck Henry and Calder Willingham or *Chariots of Fire* (1981) by Colin Welland, or a popular contemporary novel, e.g. *The Curious Incident of the Dog in the Night-Time* (2003) by Mark Haddon, *The Colour Purple* (1985) by Alice Walker or *The Kite Runner* (2003) by Khaled Hosseini. Managements commission and programme adaptations because it is easier to estimate what the box office return is likely to be if the title is already popular in another medium. A successful adaptation will allow the theatre to take risks elsewhere in its programme.

Theatres that accept unsolicited submissions from unproduced playwrights seldom accept adaptations, neither do competitions. More often than not, theatres commission adaptations from writers they have already worked with or writers who have some track record. If, however, you have had a brilliant idea about how to adapt a popular story for the stage that no one else has thought possible, and you can secure the stage adaptation rights, then it's worth having a go and taking it to a company. My award-winning adaptation of Albert Lamorisse's silent French film *The Red Balloon* (1956) was one such project.

Never adapt a story if it is still in copyright, unless you have acquired the rights to do so from the author or their agent, or the film company, or from the subject of the true story you want to tell. If the author gives you the rights, check that their agent hasn't sold them to somebody else. Raymond Briggs gave me the rights to adapt *The Snowman* for the Contact Theatre in Manchester in 1985 without realizing that he didn't, at the time, own the stage adaptation rights to his own book.

There are many different types of adaptation. The three most common are those that try, faithfully, to include all the main characters and major

The Red Balloon (1989) by Albert Lamorisse adapted for the stage by Anthony Clark with original music by Mark Vibrans, at the Contact Theatre.

events of the story, those that don't do this but stay true to the spirit of the original and those that use the original as inspiration for something that clearly owes a lot to it but to all intents and purposes is a new play. Lynne Nottage's play *Ruined* (2008), set in the Congo, very loosely mirrors Brecht's *Mother Courage and Her Children* (1939), which is set in Northern Europe during the Thirty Years War, and is an example of this type of adaptation.

Being faithful to the original source does not mean you have to slavishly adhere to every twist of the plot, or to the locations. It does not mean that you are prohibited from inventing dialogue or getting rid of, or inventing, new characters. It means that you have only invented new material to capture what you understand to be the spirit of the original.

If you love the original material and know it well enough to interpret it, ask yourself what new insights are you bringing to the material by adapting it for the stage.

Adapting something can provide you with a brilliant opportunity to experiment stylistically. Adapting for the stage often involves you having to be ingenious with the resources available to you – not only condensing a large amount of information into an hour and a half, but creating dialogue and incidents to convey that information dramatically. The cast size you will be offered will inevitably be smaller than the number of characters you are having to include, therefore the scenes need to be arranged in such a way that the actors can multi-role without it being confusing. The goal of a good adaptation is that it should speak directly to a contemporary audience and they don't have to know the original to enjoy what you have created.

Adaptation is great work if you can get it. If the material is out of copyright, you will be paid the same amount as you would for an original play. If the material is still in copyright, you will have to share

Asif Kahn in *Paradise of the Assassins* (2016) by Anthony Clark, premiered at the Tara Arts Theatre, London.

your royalty with the original author – their percentage share will invariably be larger than yours.

It's good work when you can get it. Many writers live off adaptations.

VIDEO GAMES

Writers for the stage are increasingly attracted to the idea of writing video games to supplement their income. In recent times, video games have replaced music as the most important aspect of youth culture. Game writers, however, don't just sell their idea and watch game designers bring it to life with stunning animations and interactive gameplay. They are more often than not brought into the process after a project director and their team of designers and technical wizards have developed a concept. Their role is secondary to others. If you are going to write games, you have to accept that you are part of this design team, contributing ideas for the world of the game, perhaps, and plots with endless possibilities because the gamer may build their own story, characters and dialogue. The dialogue is often foreign or made up. If you are serious about writing for games you need to play them, all types, and familiarize yourself with the technical possibilities of this interactive medium. There are plenty of excellent industry books on the subject.

TRANSLATIONS

Apart from late-nineteenth-century translations of the naturalistic dramas of Ibsen, Chekhov, Strindberg, Gorky and a handful of others, and the works of Molière and Lorca, there is a surprising reluctance to engage with non-British plays in this country. Contemporary plays from the English-speaking world (America and Australia) and the occasional popular French play by the likes of Yasmina Reza or Florian Zeller will get produced, but very few plays from across Europe, and even fewer from Africa, South America and South-East Asia. In a global world, and a multicultural society, you would think that in the interests of integration there was a real imperative to do plays in translation.

There is an ongoing debate amongst academic linguists and those that commission stage translations as to whether you need somebody with dramatic skills who can write dialogue or somebody who can speak the original language to do the job for you. Most translations that get produced are by established playwrights, working from a literal translation. There are notable exceptions like Michael Frayn who speaks Russian, and Martin Crimp, Christopher Hampton and Ranjit Bolt who all speak French.

Most translations, therefore, tend to be 'versions of' or 'adapted from' the original play. They tend to reflect more of the voice of the adapter, who will claim to be more in tune with the sensibilities of the target audience than the original playwright. It seems as long as the translation tries to produce the same effect on the audience as the play would have had on its native audience, the adapter will feel at liberty to cut and add lines. It does seem unethical, however, if this results in transposing the setting and period of the play. Learning about other cultures, their preoccupations, their mannerisms and their history is important to our understanding of our place in the world. Anything that enhances our global awareness can help us accept diversity and encourage us to shift our focus from competing with each other to preserving this planet for everybody.

If, as a playwright, you are proficient in another language, you can learn from translating a play that has stood the test of time. It is useful, sometimes, to have two plays on the go: one an original play and one a translation. When you get stuck on the first, you can hop to the second. The time away from the problem often helps you to find a way to resolve it.

If you're going to have a go at translating a popular contemporary play, make sure the rights are available.

Annie Domingo,
Sara Mair Thomas
and Joan Williams in
Blood Wedding by
Garcia Lorca in a new
translation by Gwynne
Edwards (1987)
premiered at the
Contact Theatre.

WRITING FOR CHILDREN

A child is a young human being below the age of puberty. Children's theatre is theatre that uses children's experience, conscious and subconscious, as inspiration for its creation.

Aside from pantomimes and versions of popular fairy tales at Christmas time, adaptations of best-selling contemporary children's fiction, and musicals based on child-friendly films, there is very little original theatre for children in the UK. Most theatre companies programme work for children during their school holidays as a way of making money, not because they have a passion to engage young minds by entertaining and educating them. Not because they want children to recognize, collectively, what they already know, and to introduce them to new worlds and experiences, but because they have some strange notion that they are building the audiences for the future by simply getting them into the theatre. Children are an audience in their own right; they must be spoken to directly and treated seriously.

The phrase children's theatre means different things to different people. It can describe plays performed by youngsters under the age of puberty, or it can imply theatre produced by adults for children to watch. More often than not it refers to the latter. Children have far less difficulty suspending their disbelief when they see an adult playing a child, persuasively, than an adult does. A good play can lead a child, as it leads an adult, to a significant moment of insight. It can be a way of helping a child cope with unsettling experiences.

There are some terrible assumptions made about children in so much of what passes as children's theatre. Children are not all the same. Their attention span is not limited to a matter of minutes if they are engaged by what you are presenting them with. They don't necessarily enjoy frantic storytelling by over-energized adult actors with funny voices. They are happy to listen if you have something interesting to tell them. Think about how long a child will play with a favourite toy, and how responsive and fertile their imaginations are. Not all children like bright colours and being spoken

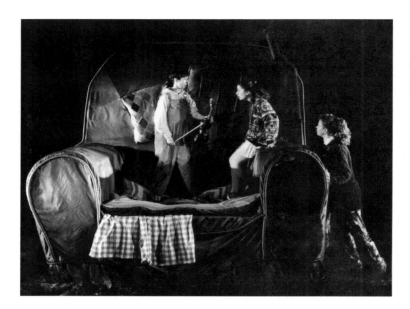

Sally Martin, Kate Somerby and Vicki Pepperdine in *The Day After Tomorrow* by Roel Adams, translated by Noel Clark, an inventive play about sibling rivalry produced at the Cottesloe, National Theatre in 1993.

to as though they won't understand what you're saying to them. A children's play doesn't have to have a moral or self-improving message. The story doesn't have to have an uplifting conclusion, as long as the writing engages their attention.

The world of a children's play can often be more imaginative than that of an adult play. Many children's plays are set in places that can become a microcosm of the real world – for example, in a toy cupboard, farmyard or on a plate full of food. You can give inanimate objects life, and animals and fantasy characters can have thoughts and emotions. You can have fun exploring human characteristics within the framework of a non-human world.

Choose contrasting characters, easily distinguishable one from the other, each having a definite function in your story. If the protagonist of your play is a child, or something, or a creature

The Red Balloon at the Contact Theatre in 1989.

Ben McKay and Nicolas Figgis in *The Maths Tutor* (2003) by Clare McIntyre, a play that explores accusations of child molestation. Premiered at Hampstead Theatre.

embodying the characteristics of a child, there are advantages to starting your play with them. As an audience, we are drawn to follow the story of the first person we see on stage until we are asked to forget them in favour of somebody else.

Think about the story and plot the same way you would think about them for an adult play. What do your characters want? What are the things that get in the way of what they want? What is threatening their world? How do they overcome it? Consider changes of fortune for your characters. As for language, let your characters speak in a variety of styles that best befit their personalities. The choice of vocabulary is important but, by the same token, don't talk down to your audience. Let them reach for the meanings of words.

If you are going to ask them to participate, make sure that what you are asking them to do is connected to the storytelling. So much audience participation during children's shows is to do with controlling the audience – whipping the kids into some sort of frenzy, so that they will sit still for the next half hour.

There are only two building-based theatre companies dedicated to producing work for children in this country: The Unicorn Theatre and Polka, and both are in London. There is, however, a range of touring companies who specialize in this work, and most regional theatres will try to programme work for this constituency once or twice a year.

WRITING FOR YOUNG PEOPLE

A young person is a person who is not a child but doesn't yet have the right to vote.

Young people's theatre tends to reflect the concerns of teenagers very directly. Plays are specially commissioned to look at subjects like self-esteem and body image, bullying, cyber addiction, gender identity, sex, drugs, alcohol abuse, racism, parental pressure, climate change and war. In the late twentieth century, there used to be a network of small-scale companies of professionally trained actor/teachers often attached to larger theatre companies, who would take issue-based work into schools. They were called TIE Companies (Theatre in Education Companies). Their work had a clear educational objective, and they were a resource for their local schools. The presentation of a play might be the centrepiece of their visit, but this would often be preceded by a workshop with the target audience and a follow-up discussion. The exploration of the issues was always from a range of different viewpoints (although it was often accused of having a left-wing bias, and some blame this for its demise). Narration was often used in the plays and they were rarely entirely naturalistic because the actors would have to multi-role, and the sets and costume, because the work was touring, tended to be simple and representational. A lot of well-established playwrights started their careers writing for TIE companies.

There are still some independent companies that do this work, but there is far less of it about. Plays for this audience do get produced as part of a theatre's main programme from time to time, but usually in the studio theatres and not on the main stage. Not all schools have the money to bring parties of young people to the theatre, unless they can get their parents to pay for the trip. Not all parents are in a position to do this.

More often than not plays for this age group are devised by, or written for, youth theatres. If you are interested in writing for this age group, make contact with your local youth theatre.

There are a number of specialist children's play publishers, many of whom act as licensees of amateur productions.

WRITING COMEDY

What causes laughter? There is no generally accepted definition of stage comedy. What one person might find funny, another will cringe at. The targets for comedy shift, depending on the sensibilities of the times. Comedy is used to explore taboo subjects. You can't guarantee that you won't offend someone, but if they are offended and you have been true to your conscience and your sense of taste, the chances are the problem is more likely to be theirs than yours. Comedy gives us insights into manners and ways of society. It tends to concern itself with the little foibles and eccentricities of human behaviour.

Characters in a comedy, like in any other play, can be one-dimensional stereotypes or complex individuals. They all have to have needs. A comic writer will put these characters in situations where they stand to lose a lot if they don't get what they need and feel they deserve. Comedy occurs when things go wrong for your characters. A lot of comedy derives from a character's inflexibility, their inability to adapt to new circumstances.

Things are funny on stage because we can see them coming, and they are funny when they are unexpected. They are funny when they are familiar and they are funny when they unfamiliar. Safe in the knowledge that what is happening on stage is not happening to us, but could, we laugh at the misfortune of others. Laughter is believed to be a form of release from our subconscious anxieties and essential for our well-being. Laughter in the theatre is infectious – it can unify an audience.

Comedies are full of misunderstandings, puns and wordplay, jokes, sarcasm, irony and satire. Some are peppered with slapstick – clumsy physical activity that exceeds the boundaries of normal behaviour. Parodies, in which a play deliberately mimics another, in order to make fun of it, are also popular.

Bertie Carvel on Paul Slack with Laura Rogers and Rachel Sanders looking on in Stephen Lowe's farce, *Revelations* (2003) premiered at Hampstead Theatre.

However funny the comedy is on the page, some actors can't realize this on stage, while others can. It is a mysterious thing and it might seem contradictory, but an actor has to play the truth of a line, whilst at the same time knowing the effect should be to make people laugh. It is all in the timing. A good comic actor like Rowan Atkinson, can take a class register in his School Master Sketch, and have the audience rolling in the aisles.

Some playwrights feel that they can't write comedy because they can't write jokes. Most jokes are two distinct ideas that come together to form one. Your mind starts with an idea and then generates and appraises other ideas for a humorous connection with the original.

There are plenty of good books on comedy writing, and plenty of good comedies to read. Remember, the audience are the only true judge of whether what you write is funny or not.

FARCE

Farce gives us insights into the mechanics and involuntary way some people behave in the pursuit of love, sex, money and status. Farce is about the anxieties people have about possible lapses of behaviour when exposed to temptations of various sorts. It usually involves extreme characters in preposterous circumstances that become more and more ludicrous until they spiral out of control.

THE WRITER'S VOICE

I write only because
There is a voice within me
That will not be still.

Sylvia Plath (1932–1963)

'Voice' is a nebulous concept talked about a lot more in relation to the novel than plays. When people talk about a playwright having a particular voice, they mean that they have identified a certain flair and originality in your writing. They can tell

your script apart from someone else's. Your writer's voice is an expression of 'you' on the page. It's about the attention you pay to what's going on around you and how you communicate your unique vision. It's about what you choose to write about and the way you choose to write about it.

The only way to find your voice is to find out who you are as a writer. Can you discern a consistency of vision and style in your work? Are they yours, or do they belong to a writer you admire? Are you intimidated by concerns of structure? Are you writing about something because it's a subject you really want to explore, or because you feel you ought to write about it? Do you have opinions? Do you own those opinions? Can they be supported by experience and/or research? Are you really taking an active interest in your surroundings? If you want others to pay attention to you, how much attention are you paying to their world? How does this attention manifest itself in your work?

Your voice is all about honesty and courage. If it is not immediately apparent in what you write, keep writing. See and read as many plays as you can, and not just those you feel that you ought to see and read. In your early drafts, try and let go of notions about the right way to do things. Let go of perfection. Always read your work out aloud whilst you are rewriting and editing.

Remember that technical proficiency is not enough to get your script accepted. What a reader wants to see is personality.

Exercises

Exercise 1 Comedy: Writing a Joke

A:

- Select a topical subject from the news.
- Write twenty factual statements about it.
- Treat each factual statement as a punchline.

B:

- Make a list of fifty funny nouns.
- Divide the list into two columns: one column has twenty nouns and the other thirty.

- *Go down the first list and make each word the subject of a joke, combining it with one of the words from the second list.*
- *Make each word in the first list the subject of your joke. Combine it with one the words in the second list to help you make a punchline.*

Example:

1. Gossip
2. Bedside light
3. Odour eater
4. Goat

27. Cauliflower
28. Vase
29. Prune
30. Hat

I like to sleep with the beside light on. I don't know why; it makes a great hat.

Exercise 2 Comedy

Write a scene with two familiar characters in a familiar situation. They are joined by a third with unpredictable consequences.

Exercise 3 Finding your Voice

- *Describe yourself in three adjectives. Ask at least two other people to describe you in the same way. Compare adjectives. Where they concur, ask yourself if these qualities are reflected in your writing.*
- *Imagine your ideal audience member. Describe them in some detail. Can you match your writing to this person?*
- *List the playwrights you like and the qualities in their writing that you admire. Where is your work similar? Where does it differ? This is not about copying your favourite playwright, it is about acknowledging your influences and aspirations.*
- *Do some free writing (writing without worrying about who it's for – stream of consciousness writing) and then compare it with something you have already written. What are the differences? Do the pressures of the writing with a particular purpose within a given structure get in the way of you expressing yourself? If you feel that they do, change both.*
- *Think of your favourite celebrity interviewer. Write down five questions you would like them to ask you about your writing, and then answer them.*
- *Your plays may include characters with different perspectives on a given subject, but the themes you have chosen to write about are yours. Can you identify them? Do you know why you've chosen them?*

APPENDIX WRITER'S CHECKLIST

- If you are writing a particular genre, are you fulfilling expectations?
- Who is your target audience?
- What is your premise? What is your play about?
- Where is your inciting incident?
- How early do you introduce your main characters?
- Do all your characters have a super-objective? And what stands in the way of them getting what they want?
- Is your dialogue governed by the way your characters think?
- Is there enough variation in pace in the dialogue? Read it aloud.
- What's the balance between showing and telling?
- Do all your characters have a role to play in the dramatic action?
- Do all your characters have a journey? An arc?
- Does your timeline make sense?
- How are you generating atmosphere in each scene?
- How are your locations contributing to the scenes?
- Make sure your present story is as compelling, if not more compelling, than the past.
- Edit your stage directions to what is essential and don't describe the way a line should be delivered.
- Is there enough variation in the tone and size (how many people on stage) from scene to scene?
- Make sure you anchor your dialogue to action. That there is something going on in each scene.
- Check your spelling and notation.
- Check your formatting is clear.

LIST OF PUBLISHERS AND AGENTS

PUBLISHERS

Aurora Metro: www.aurorametro.com
Bloomsbury Methuen Oberon Drama: www.bloomsbury.com/academic/academic-subjects/drama-and-performance-studies
Faber & Faber: www.faber.co.uk
Josef Weinberger Plays: www.josef-weinberger.com
Lazy Bee Scripts: www.lazybeescripts.co.uk
Nick Hern Books: www.nickhernbooks.co.uk
Playdead Press: www.playdeadpress.bigcartel.com
Samuel French: www.samuelfrench.co.uk
Smith Scripts: www.smithscripts.co.uk

UK AGENTS

42M&PLtd: www.42mp.com
The Agency (London Ltd): www.theagency.co.uk
Alan Brodie Representation Ltd: www.alanbrodie.com
Andrew Mann Literary Agency: www.andrewmann.co.uk
Berlin Associates: www.berlinassociates.com
Casarotto Ramsay & Associates Ltd: www.casarotto.co.uk
Curtis Brown Group Ltd: www.curtisbrown.co.uk
David Higham Associates Ltd: www.davidhigham.co.uk

Elaine Steel: www.elainesteel.com
Felix de Wolfe: www.felixdewolfe.com
Gemma Hirst Associates: www.gemmahirst.co.uk
Independent Talent Group Ltd: www.independenttalent.com
Jill Foster Ltd (JFL): www.jflagency.com
Judy Daish Associates Ltd: www.judydaish.com
Julia Tyrell Management: www.jtmanagement.co.uk
The Lisa Richards Agency: www.lisarichards.co.uk
Kitson Press Associates: www.kitsonpress.co.uk
The Knight Hall Agency Ltd: www.knighthallagency.com
MacFarlane Chard Associates Ltd: www.macfarlane-chard.co.uk
Macnaughton Lord Representation: www.mlrep.com
MBA Literary and Script Agents: www.mbalit.co.uk
Micheline Steinberg Associates: www.steinplays.com
The Production Exchange: www.theproductionexchange.com
Rochelle Stevens & Co.: www.rochellestevens.com
Sayle Screen Ltd: www.saylescreen.com
Troika: www.troikatalent.com
United Agents LLP: www.unitedagents.co.uk

NEW WRITING VENUES AND COMPANIES

ArcolaTheatre: www.arcolatheatre.com

Birmimgham Repertory Theatre (The Door): www.birmingha-rep-co.uk

Bush Theatre: www.bushtheatre.co.uk

Everyman & Playhouse Theatres: www.everymanplayhouse.com

Finborough Theatre: www.finboroughtheatre.co.uk

Graeae: www.graeae.org

Hampstead Theatre: www.hampsteadtheatre.com

HighTide: www.hightide.org.uk

Leeds Playhouse: www.leedsplayhouse.org.uk

Live Theatre: www.live.org.uk

National Theatre: www.nationaltheatre.org.uk

National Theatre of Scotland: www.nationaltheatrescotland.com

National Theatre Wales: www.nationaltheatrewales.org

The Orange Tree Theatre: www.orangetreetheatre.co.uk

Out of Joint: www.outofjoint.co.uk

Paines Plough: www.painesplough.com

Royal Court Theatre: www.royalcourttheatre.com

Royal Exchange Theatre, Manchester: www.royalexchange.co.uk

Soho Theatre: www.sohotheatre.com

Theatre 503: www.theatre503.com

Traverse Theatre: www.traverse.co.uk

This list is a partial list. Read reviews and the industry newspaper, The Stage, regularly, to keep up with venues and companies that accept submissions.

RECOMMENDED READING

Aristotle, *The Poetics* trans, Kenneth McLeish (Nick Hern Books, 1999)

Ayckbourn, Alan, *The Crafty Art of Playmaking* (Faber & Faber, 2004)

Billington, Michael, *One Night Stands: A Critic's View of Modern British Theatre* (Nick Hern Books, 1993)

Billington, Michael, *State of the Nation: The British Theatre Since 1945* (Faber & Faber, 2007)

Booker, Christopher, *The Seven Basic Plots: Why We Tell Stories* (Continuum, 2004)

Bradwell, Mike, *Devising and Directing for the Theatre* (Nick Hern Books, 2012)

Brodie, Geraldine, *The Translator on Stage* (Bloomsbury Academic, 2017)

Carlson, Marvin, *Theories of the Theatre* (Cornell University Press 1993)

Dromgoole, Dominic, *The Full Room* (Methuen, 2000)

Edgar, David, *How Plays Work* (Nick Hern, 2009)

Edgar, David, *State of Play* (Faber & Faber, 1999)

Egri, Lajos, *The Art of Dramatic Writing* (Wildside Press, 1946)

Foxon, Chris & Turvey, George, *Being a Playwright [A Careers Guide]* (Nick Hern Books, 2018)

Goldman, Lisa, *The No Rules Handbook for Writers* (Oberon Books, 2012)

Hayman, Ronald, *How to Read a Play* (Grove Press, 1999)

Horace, *Ars Poetica*

Lamott, Anne, *Some Instructions on Writing and Life* (First Anchor Books, 1995)

Mamet, David, *Writing in Restaurants* (Faber & Faber, 1986)

McKee, Robert, *Story* (Methuen, 1997)

Nelson, Richard & Jones, David, *Making Plays* (Faber & Faber, 1995)

Ramsay, Peggy, *Peggy to Her Playwrights. The Letters of Margaret Ramsay, Agent* (Oberon Books, 2018)

Sierz, Aleks, *In-Yer-Face Theatre* (Faber & Faber, 2001)

Stafford-Clark, Max, *Letters to George* (Nick Hern Books, 1989)

Stephens, Simon, *A Working Diary* (Bloomsbury, 2016)

Truby, John, *The Anatomy of Story* (Faber and Faber, 2007)

Vogler, Christopher, *The Writer's Journey: Mythic Structure for Writers* (Michael Wiese, 1992)

Waters, Steve, *The Secret Life of Plays* (Nick Hern Books, 2010)

Wright, Nicholas, *99 Plays* (Methuen, 1992)

Writers and Artists Yearbook (Bloomsbury Annual Publication)

Yorke, John, *Into the Woods: How Stories Work and Why We Tell Them* (Penguin, 2013)

INDEX